Also by Michael Lee Pope

Ghosts of Alexandria (The History Press, 2010)

Hidden History of Alexandria, D.C. (The History Press, 2011)

Shotgun Justice: One Prosecutor's Crusade Against Crime and Corruption in Alexandria and Arlington (The History Press, 2012)

Wicked Northern Virginia

Michael Lee Pope

The History Press

Published by The History Press
Charleston, SC 29403
www.historypress.net

First published 2014

Manufactured in the United States

ISBN 978.1.62619.101.3

Library of Congress Cataloging-in-Publication Data

Pope, Michael Lee.
Wicked Northern Virginia / Michael Lee Pope.
pages cm
Includes bibliographical references.
ISBN 978-1-62619-101-3
1. Virginia, Northern--History, Local--Anecdotes. 2. Virginia, Northern--Social conditions. 3. Virginia, Northern--Biography. 4. Crime--Virginia, Northern--History. 5. Corruption--Virginia, Northern--History. I. Title.
F232.N867P67 2014
975.5'9--dc23
2014035073

Notice: The information in this book is true and complete to the best of our knowledge. It is offered without guarantee on the part of the author or The History Press. The author and The History Press disclaim all liability in connection with the use of this book.

Contents

Acknowledgements

- Hope Nelson, my lovely bride, my best friend and my partner in crime.
- George Combs, for helping me navigate Alexandria Local History Special Collections.
- Julie Downie, for helping me translate Victorian euphemisms.
- Mary Fishback, for helping me navigate the Thomas Balch Library.
- Ruth Lincoln Kaye, for spreading an infectious interest in hidden history.
- Ted Pulliam, for helping me whip this wicked project into shape.

Introduction

Northern Virginia Confidential

Northern Virginia is not a state. It's barely even a coherent region, sprawling across both sides of the Fall Line. Urban and rural. Rich and poor. Old money and new greed. It has the ego of a conceited cavalier and the charm of a strip mall. The classic Virginia gentleman may live on in myth, but the reality is not as righteous.

In fact, it's pretty *wicked*.

Some version of the word "wicked" appears in the Bible about five hundred times. Wickedness caused the flood that destroyed the world, and it brought a fiery destruction to Sodom. It's associated with outrageous offense, annihilating anarchy, bitter provocation, rampant harlotry, worthless lives and pagan gods. It's silenced and smited, subordinated and slain.

But it remains with us.

Our friends from up North use it for emphasis, as in "This is a *wicked* good book." But that's not the word's only claim to fame. The original Broadway production of *Wicked* earned ten Tony nominations. And David Lynch used Chris Issac's 1989 song "Wicked Game" as a haunting refrain for *Wild at Heart*.

The story of wickedness in Old Dominion is a tale as old as human history. It stretches back twelve thousand years to the first people, a series of tribes that battled for dominance and empire. John Smith arrived on the scene with his own brand of English wickedness. It remains with us hidden in Northern Virginia today, lurking in its avenues, its alleys, its dumps, its mansions, its hotels, its police stations, its jails, its courts, its closets and its catacombs.

A tour of wicked Northern Virginia has it all—murder, mayhem, sex, violence and politics. Lots of politics. Virginia senator John Randolph dueled with Henry Clay in Northern Virginia after the two traded insults on the Senate floor. Nazi leader George Lincoln Rockwell ran for governor from his Northern Virginia headquarters. Members of the Fairfax County Board of Supervisors spent time in jail after selling their power and influence.

And yet the politics of Northern Virginia are just as divided as the opposite sides of the Fall Line. These days, it's red versus blue. But in the not-too-distant past, it might have been pushy commercial interests versus a laid-back Jeffersonian ideal. Hotheaded secessionists versus levelheaded dealmakers. Progressive reformers versus machine power.

Look beyond the bucolic story of plantation estates and you'll find one of the dizziest and dirtiest places in the world. It's a cookie full of arsenic on a cold platter of revenge. It's a region that has no industry but one: government. And it stars a rotating cast of greedy supervisors, vainglorious senators, bullying occupiers, party bosses and bloodthirsty doctors.

Chapter 1

Nine Pints

Bleeding the General at Mount Vernon

George Washington's doctors had blood on their hands.

Did George Washington's doctors kill him? Ask the tour guides at Mount Vernon and you're likely to get a swift "no" accompanied by the evil eye. But do a little digging and you'll realize the truth is a little more complicated. And bloody.

In the last twenty-four hours of his life, Washington's doctors removed nine pints of blood from his body. On a good day, a human body has about fourteen pints. That means his crackpot medical team of postcolonial quacks removed more than half of the general's blood in the final hours of his life. It's impossible to give a full medical verdict on whether bloodletting caused Washington's death, but it certainly didn't help.

Our story begins on a cold winter day—Thursday, December 12, 1799. The general, who was then a sixty-seven-year-old former president, rode out to inspect the

Did George Washington's doctors kill him? *Courtesy of the Library of Congress.*

farms on the periphery of his sprawling Mount Vernon estate. Under a cold and cloudy sky, the general mounted his trusty steed and headed out at about 10:00 a.m. to mark trees to be removed from the estate. About three hours into his tour, the sky opened up and a driving rain began, followed by hail and snow. As Washington pressed onward, the weather deteriorated. An icy December wind began to blow.

By the time he returned to Mount Vernon at 3:00 p.m., his hair was covered in snow, and his neck was soaking wet. He entered Mount Vernon at the west entrance, where he was greeted by his friend and estate manager Tobias Lear, a New Hampshire native who had started working for the Washingtons in 1784. The general went to the dining room, where the table was set for two. Lear asked Washington if he wanted to change into dry clothes, but the general was known for his punctuality and didn't like being late. He was also in a hurry to take care of some correspondence. Besides, he said, his greatcoat had kept him dry during his five-hour ride.

Still in his wet clothes, Washington warmed himself by the burning birch log in the ornate fireplace. Lear ordered a maid to bring dinner and inform Martha Washington that the general had arrived. A few minutes later, a servant girl arrived with hot tea, baked chicken and several thick slices of bread. Martha scurried into the room and began reprimanding the general for staying out in the stormy weather. She sat at the table with him as he ate, sipping tea and catching up on the day's events.

Tobias Lear. *Courtesy of Mount Vernon.*

Washington's dentures were bothering him, so he ate slowly. Then he launched into a sneezing fit. The general admitted to Martha that he was exhausted and told her that he wanted to turn in for the night. But as he was walking up the stairway to the second floor, he realized he was having difficulty breathing and that his throat felt scratchy.

"In the evening," Lear would later recall, "he appeared as well as usual."

By the time dawn broke on Friday morning, three inches of snow covered the ground at Mount Vernon. The weather had cleared by mid-afternoon, and Washington walked down the hill to the hanging wood area on the east side of the mansion and marked some trees for removal to open up the slope facing the Potomac River.

By the time he returned, his voice had become noticeably hoarse. He ate dinner and then withdrew to the parlor. Lear encouraged him to take something for his throat. Washington made light of it as usual. The general never took anything for a common cold.

"Let it go as it came," Washington responded.

In the parlor, he sat with Martha Washington and Tobias Lear reading a stack of papers from the post office in Alexandria. Lear later described Washington as remarkably cheerful that evening as the two read aloud to each other from the papers. But as time wore on, the general had difficulty speaking. So Lear began reading from debates in the Virginia General Assembly. Legislators had recently selected Wilson Cary Nicholas to fill the Senate seat now vacant after the death of Henry Tazewell. They had also selected former French ambassador James Monroe to be the next governor of Virginia, replacing Federalist James Wood. Washington had publicly criticized Monroe's support of revolutionary France during the Adams administration, and whenever Lear mentioned the governor-elect that night, Washington would respond with raspy displeasure.

His throat continued to bother him, and his voice eventually cracked and was reduced to a whisper. So he rose to his feet, stretched his arms and quietly announced that he was retiring for the evening. The general ascended the back stairwell toward his bedroom, where he climbed into the oversized canopied bed—one that could fit his massive frame.

The bedroom was a luxurious retreat. A shaving stand stood on one wall and a lady's writing desk on the other. Both had been purchased a decade earlier from French ambassador Comte de Moustier. On the other side of the room, a fire burned in the fireplace as Washington fell asleep.

Shortly after 2:00 a.m., he complained to Martha that he was suffering "an ague," essentially a violent attack of fever and shivering. Over the years, Washington had battled malaria a number of times. The previous summer, in fact, he had lost twenty-four pounds due to a malarial attack. Martha wanted to get up and call for a servant, but her husband would not allow her to do so, fearing that she might take cold. As soon as the sun rose, Martha sent a servant named Caroline to tell Lear that Washington was very ill.

Lear quickly put on his clothes and hustled to Washington's bedchamber. When he arrived, Washington was breathing heavily and barely able to

The bed where George Washington died. *Courtesy of the Library of Congress.*

speak. In a gravelly voice, Washington recounted how he had awakened at about 2:00 a.m. and found his throat was much worse. Lear immediately sent a servant named Charles to summon Dr. James Craik, "ordering him to go with all the swiftness his horse could carry him."

While they were waiting for Craik to arrive, Lear summoned Union Farm overseer George Rawlins, a bloodletter and veterinarian. Meanwhile, Lear prepared a concoction of molasses, vinegar and butter to help Washington's throat. It didn't work. Washington was unable to swallow a drop. Every time he tried, the general became distressed, convulsed and almost suffocated. Lear knew it was time for something serious.

When Rawlins arrived, the bleeding began.

To the modern mind, the idea of bleeding is more than slightly repulsive. How could people have possibly thought this was a way to make someone feel better? In reality, though, this was an era when phlebotomy—the medical art of bleeding—was common wisdom. As a result, bloodletting was practiced to the point of putting the patient in a coma. The prominent medial minds of the late eighteenth century—men such as Dr. Benjamin Rush—advised extensive bleeding for almost every

Bloodletting lancet in the collection of the Alexandria Stabler-Leadbeater Apothecary Museum. *Courtesy of Liz Lynch.*

disease. The practice of bleeding, also known as depletion therapy, was sometimes an effort to balance the "humors" of the body. Other times, it was simply an effort to rid the body of toxins. The practice had ancient roots and was still quite popular in Washington's day.

So it was really no surprise that the remedy for the general's throat problems was a good bloodletting.

At about 7:30 a.m., Rawlins started preparing Washington for the first bleeding. When the general's arm was ready, he noticed that Rawlins was agitated and could barely speak.

"Don't be afraid," Washington told Rawlins.

With that, Rawlins nicked a vein on Washington's forearm, and the bleeding began.

"The orifice is not large enough," Washington declared.

Nevertheless, crimson drops of his blood began trickling over his skin. Martha was not persuaded that bleeding was a proper remedy, though, and she begged Rawlins not to take too much blood. When he was finished, Rawlins had removed twelve to fourteen ounces of blood, about 355 to 414 milliliters.

Lear gave Washington a mixture of molasses, vinegar and butter, which brought on a bout of almost fatal choking. Martha begged them to stop, but the general reprimanded the veterinarian for taking such a small quantity of blood.

Washington's voice was reduced to a hoarse and painful whisper. Again and again, he tried to find a comfortable position for breathing as his throat continued to swell. The sound of air forcing its way through his throat filled the bedchamber. His nostrils began flaring as he struggled to fill his lungs. His skin became sallow and pale. His face was showing signs of strain.

Craik was a sixty-nine-year-old physician, trained in Edinburgh, who had frequently visited Mount Vernon. As a close personal friend of the general for more than forty-five years, Craik had been with Washington on many of his trips. He even served as an advisor to Washington during the infamous Conway Cabel incident, a time when members of Congress tried to depose Washington as commander of the colonial forces.

Washington and Craik first met during the very early days of the French and Indian War. The French had invaded from Canada and began building forts on land claimed by the British with the help of the Indians. Washington was a twenty-two-year-old colonel in the Virginia regiment. Craik was a twenty-four-year-old surgeon. The two became acquaintances whose paths would cross many times, and they would ultimately become close friends. Years later, President John Adams asked Washington to come out of retirement to become commander in chief of American forces once again, this time with the rank of lieutenant general. Washington's only condition for agreement was that Craik be named physician general.

Dr. James Craik. *Courtesy of the U.S. National Library of Medicine.*

Walking into Mount Vernon on that chilly December afternoon at about 9:00 a.m., Craik must have known the situation was serious. The first thing he did was obtain a medical history, putting together a timeline of when the symptoms started appearing and what kind of care the general had already received. By the time the doctor made his way upstairs to the bedroom, the patient's eyes were dry and lusterless. When Craik walked into the room, Washington's face flashed with recognition at the sight of his old friend. But his voice was scarcely audible when he tried to greet the doctor. In the early morning light, the doctor could see that the general's skin had a tinge of blue. He eyes were dull and dry. His eyeballs were sunken from dehydration.

Washington's lips retracted over his gums because his teeth had been removed. His hair was balding. The muscles in his neck were convulsing as he fought for breath. Washington was clearly in bad shape, and his current appearance resembled more of a death mask than the familiar image of a commanding general at his prime.

Craik was shaken at the sight of his old friend, but he got to work. The doctor took Washington's pulse while scrutinizing his face and neck. Behind him, a maid threw another log on the fire. Tobias Lear and Martha Washington stood at the back of the room, silently watching the doctor work. Craik turned to Lear and asked him to prepare some boiling water.

When the container of boiling water arrived, Craik added some vinegar and asked Washington to inhale the steam. Then he asked the patient to gargle some of the vinegar along with some sage tea. Washington's swallowing seemed to improve a bit, and he was able to take some liquids without gagging.

At 9:30 a.m., Craik applied a blister of cantharides to Washington's throat. Then, Rawlins performed a second bleeding, removing about eighteen ounces, or 532 milliliters, of blood. At 11:00 a.m., the general's condition had not improved. So Rawlins performed a third bleeding, removing another eighteen ounces of blood. All the while, Washington was gargling sage tea with vinegar, tilting his head back to drip the mixture down his throat. He nearly suffocated, though, because he was unable to cough up the fluid. Tartar emetic was administered to induce vomiting, but that didn't work either.

None of this seemed to be helping, so Craik sent for Dr. Elisha Dick and Dr. Gustavus Brown. Meanwhile, Washington beckoned for his wife with a wave of his hand and asked her to bring both of his wills. He knew that one was obsolete, and he wanted to make sure the correct one was on hand.

He handed the outdated document to Martha, who burned it in the fireplace. Through his swollen throat and parched lips, he asked Lear about

Dr. Gustavus Brown. *Courtesy of the Library of Congress.*

conditions at Mount Vernon so that his affairs could be put in order.

"I feel I am going," he said in a failing voice. "My breath cannot last long. I am near my end. It is the debt we must all pay."

Lear began moving Washington's body around in bed. "I am afraid that I shall fatigue you too much," Washington murmured. "I hope when you want aid of this kind you will find it."

The patient asked to be dressed so he could sit beside the fireplace, but he felt faint and returned to bed. A few hours later, he was felling better. Once again, he asked to be dressed so he could sit by the fireplace. But once again, he was too weak to stay, so he was helped back to bed.

At 3:00 p.m., Dr. Elisha Dick arrived. At the age of thirty-seven, Dick was a rising star in the medical profession, a man who had learned the latest medical technology in Pennsylvania and had only recently been appointed coroner of Alexandria. Dick assessed the situation and argued against another bleeding, expressing concern that it might weaken Washington.

Nevertheless, Craik overruled Dick and ordered another bleeding. At this point, Rawlins conduced a fourth and final bleeding. It was the largest amount of blood taken out of Washington all day—thirty-two ounces. That's more than twice as much taken during the first bleeding and almost double what was taken during the subsequent two.

Washington looked at Craik. "Doctor, I die hard, but I am not afraid to go," he Washington. "I believed from my first attack that I should not survive it. My breath cannot last long."

At 4:00 p.m., Dr. Gustavus Brown arrived. At the age of fifty-two, Brown was incredibly wealthy, a man from Port Tobacco, Maryland, who had trained in Edinburgh and had only recently cofounded the Medical and Chirurgical Faculty of Maryland, now known as the Maryland State Medical Society.

Dr. Elisha Cullen Dick. *Courtesy of the U.S. National Library of Medicine.*

He assessed the situation and began conferring with the medical team. But it was too late. Death was fast approaching, and everyone realized what was about to happen.

Sorrow washed over Craik's face as he gave his friend a consoling pat on the arm. Then he moved over to the fireplace, where he sat in a chair Martha placed there for him. He stared into the fire, silently contemplating the inevitable. Once again, Lear helped Washington move into a more comfortable position. Dick returned to the bedchamber and walked over to the edge of the canopied bed. Craik pulled himself from the fire and joined Dick.

"Can you sit up in bed?" Craik asked his patient.

Washington reached for Lear, who helped him to a sitting position. He sat upright but was unable to hold his head up.

"I feel myself going," he said. "I thank you for your attentions but pray you take no more trouble about me. Let me go off quietly. I cannot last long."

Lear helped him back down, and then everyone left the room except Craik and Lear. Early that evening, the doctors applied blisters and poultices of wheat bran to the patient's lower extremities. Again and again, in a weakened voice, Washington asked for the time. Sometime between 10:00 and 11:00 p.m., Washington summoned Lear. Then, in a voice that was thick and almost unintelligible, he made a final proclamation.

"I am just going," the general said. "Have me decently buried, and do not let my body be put into the casket unless I am dead three days."

Then, Washington looked sternly into Lear's eyes. "Do you understand me?" he asked.

"Yes," Lear responded.

"'Tis well," the general said.

At that point, Washington put his hand on his own pulse. His breathing had now grown weaker and weaker, gradually diminishing into shallow wheezing. His hand fell gently from his wrist. And then his breathing stopped. The general was dead.

"Is he gone?" asked Martha.

No one replied. Craik sat silently at the foot of the bed. Lear held up Washington's hand to indicate that he was no longer among the living.

"'Tis well," she said, echoing her husband's last words. "All is over now. I shall soon follow him. I have no more trials to pass through."

Full religious ceremonies and Masonic rituals were conducted four days later, in accordance with Washington's wishes. His body was placed in the family vault. Later that month, Craik and Dick published a letter to the editor of the *Alexandria Times* outlining the events of that fateful day:

> *He was fully impressed at the beginning of his complaint, as well as through every succeeding stage of it, that its conclusion would be mortal, submitting to the several exertions made for his recovery rather as a duty than from any expectation of their efficacy. He considered the operations of death upon his system as coeval with the disease; and several hours before his decease, after repeated efforts to be understood, succeeded in expressing a desire that he might be permitted to die without interruption.*
>
> *During the short period of illness he economized his time in the arrangement of such few concerns as required his attention, with the utmost serenity and anticipated his approaching dissolution with every demonstration of that equanimity for which his whole life had been so uniformly and singularly conspicuous.*

But the carefully worded letter to the editor leaves many questions unanswered, questions that have lingered for hundreds of years. Could Washington have been saved?

"In my opinion, the answer is yes," wrote Dr. Frank Pirruccello in a 1977 article for the *Chicago Tribune*.

If Washington had the benefit of modern science, he would have been taken to Inova Mount Vernon Hospital, where cultures of bacteria in his throat would have been taken, and the offending organism would have been identified. Doctors would have placed a tube through his mouth, throat and lungs to relieve his breathing. Then they would have performed a surgical procedure now known as a tracheotomy, essentially

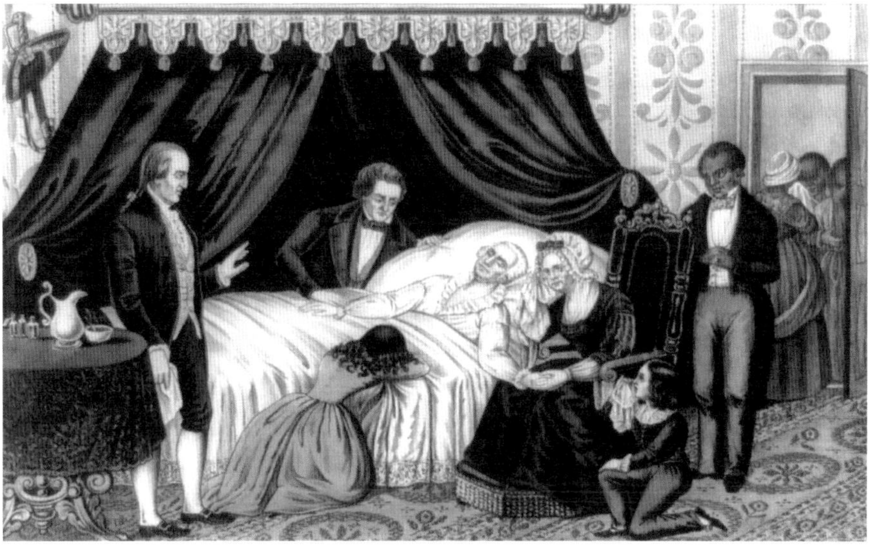

George Washington's deathbed scene. *Courtesy of the Library of Congress.*

opening a direct airway through an incision in the windpipe. If necessary, fluids would have been administered intravenously.

Antibiotics would have been ordered, and a blood transfusion would have been given. X-rays of his head and chest would have been able to pinpoint the infection. Blood counts and blood chemistry studies would have been taken. Urinalysis would have been conducted. Blood pressure would have been monitored.

But Washington had the misfortune of dying in the eighteenth century, a time when the medical arts were still clinging to the Middle Ages. Although he might have been saved by the experimental medicine that was emerging at the dawn of the nineteenth century, his doctors chose to go with the accepted practices of the day.

Dr. Dick made an effort to persuade the other doctors to perform a tracheotomy, an operation then known as a bronchotomy. But the other doctors outvoted him. Had he been successful, Dick could have made an opening in the lower neck to bypass the obstructed infection higher up in the throat.

We now know that subjecting Washington to bloodletting hastened his demise. Medical scholars who have investigated the events leading to his death estimate that he lost about half of his body's blood supply. Yes, *half* of his body's blood supply.

Mount Vernon. *Courtesy of the Library of Congress.*

"While bloodletting was not the single cause of death," wrote Pirruccello, "it was surely the element of treatment, given the state of his health, that made the outcome inevitable."

It's important to remember what the state of medical affairs was in America at the time. Of the 3,500 contemporary medical practitioners in

George Washington's tomb at Mount Vernon. *Courtesy of the Library of Congress.*

the United States, only 200 had medical degrees. Craik is generally credited with having received medical training at the University of Edinburgh, although the institution has no record of his attendance.

Although Washington's friends and doctors intended to save him, their actions directly contributed to his death. Despite the ancient credo that a physician should do no harm, it seems that's all his team of doctors were able to accomplish.

"He was methodically destroyed by the kindness of his friends, even though they were acting to the best of their judgment in the practice of medicine as it was known in the late 18th century," concluded Pirruccello. "However, had they not tried so hard to help him, it is quite possible Washington could have lived and enjoyed his retirement at Mount Vernon, which had been his fondest wish, for a much longer time."

2

Halfpenny Hitler

Nazi Power in Arlington

George Lincoln Rockwell leads Aryan Nations on Wilson Boulevard.

The name Arlington conjures images of stoic guards standing watch over the Tomb of the Unknown Soldier, but the county has a colorful past that few know much about. There's the killing ground once known as Dead Man's Hollow. And then there are the corrupt politicians who once took payoffs at a speakeasy known as Klondike Place.

But there's one chapter of Arlington's hidden history that has yet to be written. Until now.

The star is George Lincoln Rockwell, leader of the American Nazi Party. In the late 1950s, he set up shop in suburban Arlington County and operated a legion of hate. He repeatedly clashed with county leaders and police officials, moving from one ramshackle house to another as agents from the Internal Revenue Service closed in. He eventually settled at place called Hatemonger Hill and bulldozed his way into the lyrics of a Bob Dylan song. New York mayor Robert Wagner dubbed him the "Halfpenny Hitler." Rockwell's story came to a violent end one sweltering August afternoon when he was assassinated by a fellow Nazi who wanted the party to move in a socialist direction.

That was followed by a dark comedy of errors in which Nazi leaders pressed to have Rockwell—a World War II navy pilot and bonafide member of the Greatest Generation—buried at Arlington National Cemetery in his Nazi uniform. The Pentagon eventually said he could be buried at Culpepper National Cemetery, although not in the reviled uniform. The burial was aborted

George Lincoln Rockwell. *Courtesy of the Neiman Foundation for Journalism at Harvard.*

after a tense standoff between party members and police. The American Civil Liberties Union stepped in and sided with the Nazis, arguing that Rockwell should be permitted burial in his uniform if that's what he wanted.

Rockwell's body was secretly cremated, and the trial of his assassin descended into farce.

"You could easily call him hatemonger, rabble-rouser, America's most notorious anti-Semite and racist," wrote Hank Burchard, who infiltrated the group to conduct research. "But when he wanted to be, he was intelligent, witty, charming, sensitive, kind and generous."

The story begins in 1918 on a windswept farm in an Illinois community known as Bloomington. There, among the endless cornfields, George Lincoln Rockwell was born to a pair of vaudeville comedians, from whom he inherited a sense of timing and showmanship that would serve him well later in life as he pushed his message of racial hatred. Rockwell's father made a name for himself as a radio personality, living out of trunks and traveling in Pullman cars as he worked the vaudeville circuit.

His parents divorced when Rockwell was six years old. After that, he attended a series of private schools in New England and eventually enrolled at Brown University in Rhode Island, where he became the art editor of the college magazine. Then he studied at the Pratt Institute of Art in Brooklyn, honing an artistic sense that he would later use to create Nazi propaganda.

During World War II, Rockwell served as a U.S. Navy pilot. After the war, he married and started a family. He had four children and launched a career as an illustrator, receiving commissions for back cover advertisements in several national magazines. But this member of the Greatest Generation would not have the kind of family life featured in a

Nazi propaganda on display in the lobby of the headquarters at 2507 North Franklin Road. *Courtesy of the Neiman Foundation for Journalism at Harvard.*

Norman Rockwell print. Instead, when the Korean War broke out, George Lincoln Rockwell left his wife and three children and returned to military life. He was assigned to an air facility in Iceland.

This is where his life changed direction.

While serving in Iceland, Rockwell picked up a copy of Adolf Hitler's *Mein Kampf*. Reading the autobiography changed the direction of his life, and Rockwell became obsessed with Aryanism.

"It was as blinding as Saul's conversion on the road to Damascus," Rockwell would later tell a newspaper reporter.

He took an Icelandic woman as his second bride, even going so far as to honeymoon in Hitler's retreat at Berchtesgaden. In the mid-1950s, he returned to the United States and founded the World Union of Free Enterprise National Socialists. But Rockwell felt the acronym WUFENS sounded like "a wheezy dog," so he changed the name to the much more shocking and direct American Nazi Party. By 1958, Rockwell had moved the group to Arlington. In the predominantly white suburbs of the nation's capital, Rockwell would have an easier time attracting media attention. So he set up his headquarters in a brick rambler at 6512 Williamsburg Boulevard—a house owned by wealthy Baltimore benefactor Harold Arrowsmith, to whom Rockwell referred to as "my fat cat." From the street, neighbors could see a giant Nazi swastika illuminated by a red sun lamp.

"The house became an attraction," said Arlington Chamber of Commerce president Rich Doud, who was in high school at the time. "When you had out-of-town guests, you would drive by the house and show them our neighborhood Nazi."

It didn't take long before the Nazis started making news. Within a few months of the group's move to Williamsburg Boulevard, the American Nazi Party made a bomb threat against the Arlington Unitarian Church, where many Jewish congregants gathered. The Nazi group's members also publicly aligned with a Georgia racist who was indicted (but not convicted) for bombing a synagogue in Atlanta. All of this was done with a sort of charm that attracted a devoted cadre of white trash and college dropouts.

"He can be such a hell of a nice guy, you find yourself forgetting what he's trying to do," said an FBI agent assigned to keep track of the Nazi leader.

Party members also stopped vehicles traveling on Williamsburg Boulevard to conduct searches. Nazi storm troopers made a point of parading back and forth fully armed. This attracted the attention of the Arlington Police Department, which decided to do something about the nuisance. By the end of April 1959, commonwealth's attorney William Hassan arrived at the Nazi headquarters with a search warrant.

They carted out several cartons of what the prosecutor called "un-American hate literature" and several books advocating the "principles and policies of Adolf Hitler and the Third Reich of Germany," as well as a giant swastika, a hunting knife, a bronze plaque of Adolf Hitler, tear gas, two pistol belts and a tape recording of German martial music. They left several items undisturbed, including an eighty-five-pound barbell, two Bibles, a copy of *Mein Kampf* and a half-eaten birthday cake with pink frosting to celebrate Hitler's seventieth birthday earlier in the week. Dozens of neighbors

George Lincoln Rockwell reads from a Nazi brochure titled *Winston Churchill Tells the Truth About Jews*. *Courtesy of the Neiman Foundation for Journalism at Harvard.*

watched as Nazis marched in and out of the home giving the traditional *sieg heil* salute. Rockwell seized the opportunity to announce his candidacy for the Virginia state senate.

"He is now receiving the attention he has been seeking," the *Washington Post* editorialized. "The seizure by police of some of his literature and books is particularly disturbing."

The Nazi bunker attracted attention from many quarters, including students. A few weeks after the raid, a nineteen-year-old George Washington University student named Henry Burchard infiltrated the operation to write a paper on deviant subgroups. Apparently, he wasn't impressed by what he observed.

"They sat around and told anti-Jewish and anti-Negro jokes," Burchard explained. "They tried to act tough."

Burchard explained that all the participants had to have party names, which were supposed to have some kind of association with their real names. Burchard suggested "Trooper Birch," but the Nazis said that wasn't tough enough. So Rockwell dubbed the teenage infiltrator "Trooper Oak." At one point, the Nazis suspect him of being a spy, so they questioned him under a red spotlight. Then they nicked his cheek with a razor, squeezing out a drop of blood on a Nazi flag.

George Lincoln Rockwell presides over Nazi headquarters at 928 North Randolph Street. *Courtesy of the Neiman Foundation for Journalism at Harvard.*

After Arrowsmith broke with Rockwell and evicted the group from his home, the Nazis moved to a cabin in the wilderness of Spotsylvania County. That's when White Citizens Council leader Floyd Fleming purchased a frame house at 928 North Randolph Street and set up Rockwell rent-free in Arlington again.

The building included a wide array of tenants, making for some strange bedfellows. The top floor was rented out by the local bus drivers' union and the Virginia Mental Health Association. But insurance companies refused to cover the building because of the presence of the Nazis, so the bus drivers and the health group moved out. That caused real estate broker Rose Hall to tell reporters that she would be foreclosing on the Nazi tenants.

But she didn't have a chance. The Nazis raised enough money to buy the house, undercutting the need for insurance.

For many neighborhood children, the Nazi house became an object of endless fascination. Rocks and insults were hurled at the house, creating a tense situation. In the summer of 1961, thirteen-year-old Ricky Farber was walking by the house on the way home from a dance at Washington-Lee High School when he was grabbed and forced into the Nazi house. The Jewish boy was handcuffed and forced inside, where he was subjected to interrogation at gunpoint. Two of the Nazis were later sentenced to a year on the Virginia State convict chain gang for assaulting the boy.

Despite the intensity of what happened in the house, those who made it inside were often confronted with utter banality.

"What greeted me was a grubby haunted house," said New York City police investigator Tony Ulasewicz, who later became famous during the Watergate scandal. "Clearly, this was no showpiece that would attract membership into Rockwell's party."

In his memoir, Ulasewicz's description of the Randolph Street house told an unsettling story, one that might not have been apparent at first but revealed itself on closer examination.

"As I looked around, I noticed that bullet holes punctured the walls of the house," he wrote. "I also saw a pack of unpaid bills on a table; Rockwell's electricity had been turned off, and he used kerosene lamps to light the place."

When photographer Jack Hiller and reporter Zander Hollander arrived at the house in the spring of 1960 to shoot preparations for a rally, they saw guns on the wall and a noose hanging from the ceiling. They observed the way the Nazi leader demanded that guests wipe their feet on an ark curtain taken from a synagogue that Rockwell insisted on calling a "Jewish prayer rug."

"You look like a Jew," Rockwell said, noticing Hiller's horn-rimmed glasses. "Prove you're not by standing on the prayer rug and saying you hate Jews."

"I wouldn't mean it if I said it," Hiller responded.

"You're right," Rockwell shot back.

The Nazis asked Hiller to avoid taking photographs of Arrowsmith, but he snapped a few shots anyway. Meanwhile, Hollander befriended a Nazi from Texas, whom the journalists later paid to fish envelopes out of the trash so the journalists could follow the money trail and track down the donors. Hiller and Hollander eventually forwarded the list to B'nai B'rith, a Jewish community service organization that was actively tracking the Nazis.

Rockwell was well aware that he was a target. An imposing man who stood six feet, four inches tall, with piercing eyes a penetrating stare, the Nazi leader may have suffered from a mental disorder. Some say he was paranoid. Others said he was a megalomaniac. His ex-wife sought to get him into counseling, and a judge ordered Rockwell to undergo a psychiatric

George Lincoln Rockwell speaks at an Arlington School Board meeting. *Courtesy of the Neiman Foundation for Journalism at Harvard.*

evaluation at St. Elizabeth's Hospital in the District. He was found to be of sound mind.

Whatever was happening inside his mind, he certainly made an impression in public.

"My fellow Americans," is how he would typically begin his speeches on the National Mall, where hundreds of tourists would look on with disbelief.

"You're sick," the tourists would often shoot back after seeing the Nazi swastika.

"Filthy, vile Jews," he would retort.

Rockwell built the American Nazi Party into a national force for hate, one with chapters from Los Angeles and San Francisco to Dallas and Philadelphia. During the 1963 March on Washington for civil rights, Rockwell sent a lieutenant dressed in a gorilla costume. When the Mississippi Freedom Democratic Party tried to get the regular Mississippi delegation unseated from the House of Representatives, Rockwell smuggled a trooper in blackface into the well of the House. When "freedom buses" were traveling across the county, Rockwell sent a Volkswagen dubbed the "hate bus" into the Black Belt.

And yet even though the operation reached from coast to coast, the financing was murky. In his personal life, Rockwell depended on his mother for income for his entire life, according to historian Frederick Simonelli. Some said he received money from Arab governments angered by the creation of Israel. He was able to pull in some income from speaking engagements at colleges that did not shy from allowing a Nazi on campus.

Wherever the money came from, Rockwell was clearly able to hold his ragtag band of marginalized agitators together despite the financial challenges. They picketed Mario's Pizza House on Wilson Boulevard after owner Howard Levine refused the Nazis service. They trailed civil rights Freedom Fighters marching with Martin Luther King Jr. in the South, and they organized marches at nightclubs that dared to book Sammy Davis Jr. They picketed Israeli prime minister David Ben-Gurion's visit to Washington, D.C., and they demonstrated at theaters showing the movie *Exodus*.

"To my knowledge, there's just one man that's a true American—George Lincoln Rockwell," sang Bob Dylan in his song "Talkin' John Birch Paranoid Blues." "I know for a fact he hates Commies 'cuz he picketed the movie *Exodus*."

The Nazis began making themselves a regular feature of Arlington School Board meetings, wearing swastika armbands and protesting desegregation.

"You can beat the race mixers," read one of the fliers.

George Lincoln Rockwell parading in front of Mario's Pizza. *Courtesy of the Neiman Foundation for Journalism at Harvard.*

In 1965, Rockwell threw his hat into the ring for governor—a race that featured Democrat Mills Godwin and Republican Linwood Holton. Because Godwin supported President Lyndon Johnson, he lost the segregationist vote and was forced to contend with a conservative backlash in the form of William Story, a fifty-six-year-old assistant superintendent from Chesapeake City public schools who was running on the short-lived Virginia Conservative Party ticket. Rockwell rounded out the ballot, appearing as the candidate of the White Majority Party.

"Rockwell has done little more than file his petition for candidacy and send his 'storm troopers' to heckle Godwin and Holton at major campaign meetings," the *Washington Post* reported.

Godwin won the election handily, although Rockwell took about 6,000 votes out of 570,000 cast in that election. A month after losing the election, Rockwell found himself in the crosshairs of the Internal Revenue Service. Agents arrived at the Randolph Street house and seized the property for nonpayment of taxes, a bill that was about $7,000. Rockwell moved the operation to Wilson Boulevard. Because the IRS confiscated their printing equipment, the Nazis were forced to move their printing operation to a plant outside Fredericksburg.

As it turns out, Rockwell had much more to worry about than IRS agents.

On a sweltering August afternoon in 1967, Rockwell took a break from working on a book he titled *White Power* to head across the street to do his laundry at the Econowash in the Dominion Hills Shopping Center. He told the owner of the coin-operated laundromat that he had to return home to get some bleach and that he would be back in half an hour.

He never made it back, leaving behind sheets in one machine and three undershirts and two undershorts in another.

As the Nazi leader began backing up his blue 1958 Chevrolet, the sound of gunfire pierced the humid summer air. Two bullets crashed into the windshield, one hitting the Nazi in the head and another piercing his heart. Rockwell staggered out of the car, pointed toward the shopping center roof and then fell face-up in the parking lot next to a box of Ivory Snow and a copy of the *New York Daily News*. His vehicle continued to roll slowly backward, crashing into a parked car.

Within a few minutes, the leader of the American Nazi Party was gone. The cause of death was a gunshot wound to the heart.

"I was in the shop cutting a head of hair," barber James Cummings told the *Washington Post*, "when this guy fired from the top of the building."

Witnesses said they saw the sniper run along the roof and then jump down to the ground in the rear of the building. None of the eyewitnesses said they saw a gun, although police later found expended shells on the roof. They told police the shooter was wearing a trench coat and hat along with a yellow sport shirt.

"When I heard the shots, I thought a car had backfired," said Tom Blakeney, owner of the nearby Tom's Barbershop. "I saw Rockwell kind of jumping around in the front seat, and I though he was having a seizure. I saw him point at the roof and then slump over the steering wheel."

Blakeney and another barber bolted into action—running after the shooter even though they ran the risk of being shot themselves.

"I was a dummy," Blakeney later concluded. "But I wanted to see who the guy was."

He eventually came to the home of a woman he knew, so he stopped and asked to use the phone. When he got the police on the line, he explained what had happened and which direction the shooter was headed. Blakeney's call led investigators to Bon Air Park. Within half an hour, the Arlington Police Department had a suspect in custody.

As it turns out, the triggerman was not a Nazi-hater but a disgruntled fellow Nazi by the name of John Patler, a twenty-nine-year-old former marine from Harlem. He grew up in a poor Greek family that lived in a tenement, where his father shot his mother in what Patler would later describe as "a crime of passion; one of those freak episodes in life when a man permits his emotions to blind his rational thought." Since meeting Rockwell at a Nationalist Youth League meeting in 1957, Patler had been a rising star in the organization.

Until now.

He was arrested on Washington Boulevard running from a bus stop near Harrison Street. Deputy police chief Raymond "Boots" Cole saw the suspect wearing a yellow sport shirt and immediately identified him as one of the Nazi leaders he had been tracking for years. So he radioed for backup. The suspect's abandoned raincoat and hat were later found in a yard behind Dominion Hills, and his discarded pistol was discovered in Four Mile Run. The forty-year-old German Mauser semiautomatic firearm, which fired 7.63-millimeter rounds, was recovered by Arlington police officer Francis Beakes.

Patler was held on a $50,000 bond at the Arlington County Jail, where he was interrogated for hours before being placed in a heavily guarded cell. Patler's wife asked controversial former school board member Helen Lane to serve as his lawyer, a task she took on with force. By 5:00 p.m. that sweltering August afternoon, Patler had been formally charged with murder. The Nazis organized a press conference and did what Rockwell would have done: seized the opportunity for maximum publicity.

"A lot of people in the Jewish community and black community will be glad tonight that he is dead," said Mattias Koehl, the party's second in command.

Koehl said Rockwell had a premonition of his own death and that he almost never moved around by himself. But the other party leaders were out of town, so Rockwell was alone the day he died. By the time dawn was breaking the next morning, readers of the *Washington Post* were digesting this front-page news: "George Lincoln Rockwell, commander of the small, boisterous and hate-peddling American Nazi Party, was shot dead by a rooftop sniper at noon yesterday in an Arlington shopping center."

As if that was not shocking enough, what followed was a second act that had all the makings of a tragic comedy. All the vaudeville showmanship that Rockwell brought to life manifested in his death, and the events surrounding his burial displayed all the absurdity Arlington County had come to expect from the Nazi leader. Despite all his grandstanding in favor of Adolf Hitler, Rockwell was an honorably discharged veteran of World War II and Korea. The Pentagon ruled that he was entitled to burial at any of one hundred national cemeteries except Arlington, where eligibility is tightly restricted.

The family wanted a quiet burial in Boothbay Harbor, near the Maine home of Rockwell's father, the famous vaudevillian. But party leaders had other plans—a modern vaudeville pageant with full military honors, including the deceased wearing a swastika armband and party insignia. Koehl emerged in public to announce that Rockwell would be buried at Culpepper National Cemetery, founded in 1862 during the Civil War. Virginia senator

Harry Byrd Jr. asked that permission be denied, and the Culpepper unit of the American Legion tried to block access. Koehl and party leaders retreated behind closed doors to plot a standoff with military police.

Meanwhile, Patler's trial was becoming a spectacle in its own right. During one emotional Arlington County Court hearing, a twenty-one-year-old Australian named Eric Ray Wenberg lunged at the accused murderer and began yelling, "You filthy swine! Long live the American Nazi Party!" Eight sheriff's deputies leaped on Wenberg and hustled him away as he shouted, "You filthy assassin!" and "Long live Matt Koehl!"

The day of the funeral was scheduled for August 30, 1967, a Tuesday.

Nazis gathered in four cars to escort the hearse to Culpepper, a circus that included sixty military police, dozens of state and local police officers and a scrum of media types eager to capture the spectacle. About one hundred sympathizers, wives and children came out for the funeral. They endured jeers and snickers from curious onlookers, and the crowd continued to grow as the hearse bumped across the railroad tracks at the entrance of the cemetery at 10:30 a.m.

A storm trooper standing guard at the Rockwell hearse. *Courtesy of the Neiman Foundation for Journalism at Harvard.*

A chaotic funeral scene. *Courtesy of the Neiman Foundation for Journalism at Harvard.*

The frenzy of news photographers and reporters delayed the procession, and a Southern Railway freight train narrowly missed smashing into an Arlington police cruiser. Newsmen outnumbered Nazis by about five to one. Tension was building, and the temperature was rising. By the time they made it to the gates, cemetery superintendent Edward Maxwell informed Koehl that the hearse would not be allowed to proceed until the Nazis removed their armbands and set aside their Nazi flags.

"All right, folks!" belted a deputy sheriff. "Take off those armbands. If you don't, you don't come in. That's final."

The Nazis refused, which created a standoff that both sides seemed to be expecting. After about an hour or so, supporters arranged floral offerings behind the hearse. One wreath from the Canadian National Socialist Party had red carnations and white chrysanthemums, which were adorned with a ribbon that read, "Lincoln Rockwell, enter Valhalla and Guide us to victory." One arrangement featured yellow flowers in the shape of a corncob pipe, a totem that Rockwell's supporters associated with their slain charismatic leader.

As the standoff dragged on at the entrance of the Culpepper National Cemetery, the Nazis made several attempts to storm the gates. The first was shortly after noon, when storm trooper Douglas Niles led his forces by chanting, "Let him through! We want in! He is an American serviceman." But the driver did not follow orders to move forward, and Niles did a neat back flip onto the hood of the vehicle before being dragged away by authorities. Four party members were arrested, including a nineteen-year-old army soldier who gave a *sieg heil* as authorities carted him away and eventually declared him AWOL.

General Carl Turner and another squad of military police officers landed in helicopters behind the cemetery. Then, mourners looked up in amazement as five helicopters roared into Culpepper, straight from the Pentagon. Now commanding a small army of sixty military police and dozens of other officers, the fifty-four-year-old general made his way to the cemetery gates and presented Koehl with an ultimatum: ditch the Nazi paraphernalia or leave.

"The commander is entitled by right to the kind of ceremony he desired," the Nazi declared.

"I'm not discussing the matter of your ideas and beliefs," the general snapped back. "I'm telling you my instructions."

Rockwell's followers called the commanding general "a two-star phony" and "little runt" before singing the Nazi song "Horst Wessel." The trim general maintained an air of detached amusement as his tiny mustache twitched in a movement some interpreted as a smile.

"Are you waiting for anything, General?" one of the reporters asked him.

"No," he replied. "Just waiting for a cigar."

The general was handed a cigar and carefully considered his next move. Just then, a Nazi captain climbed up the rear of the hearse, stood on the top and ordered an assault on the troops blocking the way. A group of military police nabbed him, and nobody else followed suit. Koehl took off his armband and headed to the superintendent's office to see if he had changed his mind.

No, he said. He had not. At 3:30 p.m., the general finally offered an ultimatum.

"In view of your refusal to comply with regulations," the general concluded, "the Department of the Army has withdrawn approval for the burial of George Lincoln Rockwell in this cemetery or in any other national cemetery."

State police escorted the Nazi hearse back to an Arlington funeral home at sixty-five miles an hour. The family tried to gain possession of the body, but the Nazis smuggled the remains out of the funeral home and into a crematorium, bringing the ashes of the slain leader back to the shabby party headquarters on Wilson Boulevard. Then Koehl gathered newsmen for an impromptu press conference outside the barracks.

"The swastika is a symbol of our faith, not a mere political symbol," Koehl told the press. "Without the swastika, we could not perform a ceremony appropriate to the wishes of Commander Rockwell."

"It's a totally depressing, unhappy mess," responded Robert Rockwell, a brother of the deceased. "I just don't know what to do. It's bewildering."

The show trial of Rockwell's assassin was unlike any that had ever been conducted at the Arlington Circuit Court, featuring ninety-two witnesses and dramatic testimony revealing the final days of the Nazi leader. During the court hearings, photographs of Patler and Rockwell were entered into evidence. But jurors learned that the relationship between the two was strained and that Patler had an on-again-off-again relationship with the party.

Fellow Nazis called him a dark-haired "greasy Greek," and many suspected him of being a Marxist. Part of the tension was that Patler wanted to strip the American party of its German trappings. Earlier that year, he had persuaded party leaders to change the name of the organization from the American Nazi Party to the National Socialist White People's Party. He left the party and returned a couple of times; a letter found in Rockwell's wallet seemed to indicate that he was once again attempting reconciliation when the assassination happened.

Patler's defense team tried to argue that he was three miles away at the time, at his home on Lee Highway. He ran a few errands that day with his wife and child, making a purchase at Arlington Paper Supply in Clarendon before going for a walk. In an effort to counter the prosecution's case, the defense hired a high school track star to run the alleged escape route in an effort to prove the accused would not have had the time.

Commonwealth's attorney William Hassan capped weeks of testimony with a dramatic closing argument.

"I ask you to determine John Patler guilty of killing by lying in wait," the prosecutor concluded. "Give him the chair."

Patler's wife ran screaming from the courtroom when Hassan finished, a dramatic flourish to end the bizarre trial. After a four-hour deliberation, on December 15, 1967, the jury found him guilty of murder and sentenced him to twenty years in prison.

The windows of the Nazi headquarters were boarded up, and the gatepost with a swastika emblazoned on it was thrown on its side. Somebody painted a Star of David on the driveway, and the owner reclaimed the house to sell it to a developer. The property is now part of Upton Hills Regional Park.

The Nazis tried to soldier on in Arlington County, eventually settling in a brick building at 2507 North Franklin Road, a spot now occupied by the Java Shack. The Nazis shared the building with a dentist and former Arlington County Board member Lucas Blevins, who told the *Northern Virginia Sun* that he found the arrangement "nauseating."

Rockwell left behind a party in tatters and a shredded personal life. His estate didn't amount to much—$257 in cash and his trademark corncob pipe. Koehl tried to take the reins of the party and move forward, but the party

Top: Nazi headquarters at 2507 Franklin Road. *Courtesy of the Neiman Foundation for Journalism at Harvard.*

Right: Storm troopers stand guard over the spot where Rockwell was assassinated. The swastika marks the spot where Rockwell died. *Courtesy of the Neiman Foundation for Journalism at Harvard.*

suffered without its captivating and hypnotic leader. Members of the party were bitterly divided and engaged in a number of gun battles—mainly against one another.

During the bicentennial celebration, the Nazis marched in the Independence Day Parade with a swastika-decorated drum corps. On the tenth anniversary of the shooting, Koehl organized a commemorative ceremony at the spot where Rockwell died. A swastika was painted on the sidewalk of the Dominion Hills Shopping Center, which will forever be associated with the 1967 assassination.

3

Chaff Before a Whirlwind

Arsenic and Old Lace in Leesburg

Did Emily Lloyd poison her husband and four children with arsenic?

It's almost unthinkably wicked—poisoning your husband and children with arsenic and then defiantly maintaining your innocence in a court of law. And yet that's probably what happened in Leesburg back in the 1870s, a time when the region was still struggling to emerge from being on the losing end of the Civil War. The femme fatale of this story is Emily Lloyd, a seamstress who weighed about one hundred pounds with a dark complexion and small, gray eyes that were dark and expressive. She had a growing family and a life full of promise. The *Loudon Mirror* described her as being "indulgent to her children, almost to a fault." She was a member in good standing of the Episcopal Church. Neighbors considered her to be industrious and kindhearted. Her children were devoted to her.

And then it all fell apart.

The view from the inside of the Lloyd house must have been significantly different. Rumors swirled around Leesburg that her husband, Charles Lloyd, was a strong man with a violent temper. He was the keeper of a drinking saloon, and people said he was unkind to his family. But he showed up to work on time and was otherwise an upstanding citizen. So nobody thought much about him, except Emily Lloyd.

In 1868, just before Christmas, Charles Lloyd became ill. Very ill. People assumed it was typhoid fever, but then he began to recover. On one visit to the house, his physician found him sitting up, doing much better. The patient

Charles Lloyd's grave. *Photo by Michael Lee Pope.*

said he would be at the saloon the next day, and the doctor pronounced him out of danger. Sadly, this was not to be the case. Shortly after the doctor left, he had a "refreshment" supplied by his caring wife. Within an hour, he was dead.

The doctor was summoned less than an hour after he left the house, returning to find Charles Lloyd stone cold dead. The small community of Leesburg was shaken by the sudden death, but the doctor proclaimed it a disease of the heart. The next day, his remains were buried in Union Cemetery—a burial plot that was about to get very crowded very soon.

Charles Lloyd left the family—Emily and their four children, two boys and two girls—in relatively comfortable circumstances. One child was born a few weeks after her father's death. The children became idolized objects of the widow's affections.

Within a few months, Emily Lloyd's aunt would also die under mysterious circumstances. In April 1870, Mrs. Hammerly of Washington, the woman who had raised young Emily and acted as a loving and devoted mother, arrived in Leesburg for a visit. Within a few weeks of her arrival, however, the shovels were back in action at Union Cemetery, digging another grave. But the aunt was old and infirm, so her death did not raise suspicion—at

The graves of the two little Lloyd boys. *Photo by Michael Lee Pope.*

least not yet. Her death elicited little more than additional sympathy for Emily Lloyd, who was, of course, still grieving the death of her husband.

That summer, the boys went out into the wilderness to go blackberry picking. When they returned home that July evening, both boys became seriously ill. Dr. Armstead Mott, the family physician, was called to the house. He determined they were suffering from the effects of poison. Because their mouths were covered with "interruptions," the doctor concluded that they had inadvertently eaten poison oak leaves with their berries.

Their condition grew worse. The family called Dr. William Cross to help Dr. Mott. But their efforts didn't work. Both of the boys died—Henry on July 24, and George on July 25. Once again, the shovels started turning earth in Union Cemetery. Two little graves were dug. Two little bodies were interred.

Meanwhile, Emily Lloyd manifested all the evidence of sorrow natural to a maternal heart lacerated by the sudden death of her two sons. She was seen arriving every day at the grave site, bending over the fresh mounds of earth. And each time she turned her back on the graves and walked out the gates of Union Cemetery, a bunch of flowers could be seen resting on the cold mounds covering her dearly departed children.

None of that stopped the gossip mill, of course. Leesburg was now buzzing with rumor and innuendo. Several people called for an examination of the boys' stomachs, but nobody was bold enough to call foul play.

What exactly was going on at the Lloyd house?

Other than Emily Lloyd, nobody really knew the answer to that question. Although some were privately clamoring for an examination of the young boys' stomachs, nobody was willing to go public with formal charges. So no evidence was gathered, and any potential clues were buried in Union Cemetery. Meanwhile, Emily Lloyd could not stand living at the Lloyd home anymore. It was the scene of too many painful memories. So she took up residence in a neat little one-and-a-half-story stone house on the west end of Loudoun Street.

"Here it was hoped that her and her surviving little ones would be spared the withering touch of the Angel of Death, which seemed to brood like an evil genius over her household," the *Loudoun Mirror* explained. "But not so."

The single-story stone house had a steep, old-fashioned roof with shingles that were curling from age. A coat of whitewash paint covered the rough exterior, an ungainly surface of rock. The house had two windows, green shutters and a white porch, which extended out toward the sidewalk to let in the daylight. Two locust shade trees were in the yard, acting as grim sentinels guarding the entrance of the unhappy household.

On February 11, 1872, the doctor was summoned to the Lloyd house yet again. This time, it was for the eldest daughter, Annie. He found her suffering from what he thought to be the effects of cholera morbus, which he blamed on bad oysters. He administered treatment, but it didn't work. On February 16, 1872, Annie Lloyd died. The doctor pronounced the cause of death to be congestion of the stomach. The next day, Annie joined her brothers and her father six feet under at Union Cemetery—the silent city of the dead.

Once again, people started talking. Suspicion was aroused. Rumors proliferated. This time, questions were openly asked as opposed to silently whispered. And yet, nobody was willing to cast the first stone, accusing a mother of the most unspeakably horrible crime. So no one spoke up. And no charges were filed.

But it wasn't long before the dull thud of cold earth was again heard at Union Cemetery, and the Lloyd household was once again the scene of tragedy. This time, it was only remaining child, Maud, of the now devastated clan. She became sick on March 23, 1872. And then, the last lovely flower left blooming on the family tree began to wilt and slowly die. On March 25, 1872, she succumbed.

Maud's grave. *Photo by Michael Lee Pope.*

Now the flames of suspicion became an overwhelming conflagration. People were asking questions, and they wanted answers. The *Loudoun Mirror* captured the moment in classic Victorian prose:

> *The announcement of Maud's death fell upon the public with stunning effect. A mighty wrong, or a terrible fatality had fallen upon a household and swept away the last of its treasures, as ruthlessly as chaff before a whirlwind, and there came an appeal from almost every Christian heart, seconded, as it were, by a mighty voice from an unseen world, pleading in behalf of a score of new made graves, for investigation.*

Enter Richard Montgomery Bentley, a longtime railroad inspector who was working as a coroner for the Loudoun County prosecutor. He summoned a jury of inquest to get answers on Tuesday, March 26, 1872—just one day after the Maud Lloyd's death. He arrived at the Lloyd house and demanded to see the body of the girl, who was still in her lying-in bed. He examined the corpse and then set out to interview witnesses.

No charges had been filed yet, although all the parties were summoned to the courthouse for testimony. On the stand, Emily Lloyd said that the child was sick for two days before she died, although she added mournfully that her daughter did not appear to suffer much. When Maud became sick, Emily testified, the girl became very pale and began throwing up over and over again. Emily administered a product known as Frey's Vermifuge—a concoction of castor oil, aromatic syrup of rhubarb, oil of Baltimore, wormseed and croton oil. That caused Maud to pass two worms, and her appetite improved. She ate some ham and toast, and then Emily gave her only remaining daughter her last bath. She died "easily and calm" shortly afterward.

Dr. Mott was next to testify. When he first saw the child, he told the court, he did not think she was seriously ill. He gave her calomel and limewater every two or three hours, but that didn't seem to help much. She had the appearance of congestion of the stomach and was continually vomiting. On Sunday evening, he found that the girl's condition was growing worse. So he started giving her Bismuth powders, one every three or four hours. By Monday morning, the doctor found the child "oppressed with every evidence of congestion."

Dr. Mott called for Dr. Cross, and the two examined the girl together and set out a course to save her life. They administered morphine and oxalate cerium, as well as a concoction known as Huxham's tincture of bark. None of it worked, the doctor told the court. Maud died despite all their best efforts. He testified that he believed the cause of death was intense congestion, and he told the court the girl was not in pain.

In what must have been excruciatingly graphic testimony, Dr. Mott told the court in detail about what the child had vomited, which he described as "bilious" in appearance. She was not vomiting blood, he explained, and her tongue appeared normal. Dr. Mott explained to the court that he had served as the family doctor for years and that he had examined all the children—all of whom seemed to have weak stomachs. He concluded that he felt there was no reason to believe that poison was the cause of death.

Dr. William Cross took the stand next. He told the court that he was an eyewitness to the girl's death on Monday morning. He testified that when the girl was on her deathbed, he had concluded that the only possible way to save her was the use of stimulants—both internal and external—as well as antiemetics to counteract the excessive vomiting. He also told the court that he had observed her pupils to be inordinately dilated, which he concluded meant that she was showing signs of brain irritation.

Town sergeant Bernard Attwell was next on the stand. When he learned of the girl's death, he paid a visit to grocery dealer Samuel Orrison, who served as the child's guardian. Together, they agreed that a forensic examination was needed. So they walked over to the Lloyd house and

Detail of Charles Lloyd's grave. *Photo by Michael Lee Pope.*

told Emily Lloyd that they thought an examination was best for her own sake—that all of Leesburg was buzzing about the suspicious series of events leading to one death after another.

She refused. They redoubled their efforts. She refused again. So they left. But then she changed her mind, calling Attwell and Orrison to return to the Lloyd house. Attwell testified that Emily Lloyd told them that William Lloyd—brother of her dead husband—had nothing but spite for her and that she had purchased milk from him.

"That old rascal," she told Attwell, according to his testimony.

The implication was that something was wrong with the milk, leading to the death of her child. But Attwell was suspicious because Delphi, the African American servant girl, told the sergeant that all the family members drank the milk and that it didn't make her sick. Delphi was next on the stand. She told the court that she had never seen any poison in the house and had never known Emily Lloyd to be in possession of arsenic. The house didn't have a problem with rats anyway, she said, and they would have been concerned about the children getting into it.

Delphi told the court that the children never took any medicine except what was administered by their mother. The black woman told the court that she did all the dealing for Emily Lloyd and that she had never been sent to the apothecaries; nor had she ever purchased anything from druggist Thomas Edwards. She described the scene at the house as hopeful that the girl would make it through the illness until Sunday morning, when the girl's situation declined rapidly. The servant said that Emily Lloyd appeared surprised by the death and that she was "much distressed."

"This child was taken just like the last child that died," Delphi testified.

Druggist Julian Hutchinson was next to be sworn in and take the stand. He told the court he could remember only one occasion in which he sold Emily Lloyd anything. Unfortunately for the woman in black at the defendant's table, that item was one ounce of arsenic a few days before the death of her boys the previous summer.

"She said it was to poison rats," the druggist testified.

The tension in the courtroom must have been palpable at that moment because Emily Lloyd was quickly called back to the stand. She testified that although she purchased most of her medicines from Dr. Armstead Mott, she had bought arsenic and Frey's Vermifuge from Dr. Edwards about a month earlier to kill rats. Strangely, the arsenic never made its way into the house, she testified, because she somehow "lost" it on the way home.

"Rats are bad here," she testified.

She also told the court that she had purchased arsenic from Dr. Mott but never used it because she was afraid the children would get a hold of it. So, she testified, she set it on fire. She was asking the court to believe that she had lost the arsenic she purchased from Dr. Edwards and that she had burned the arsenic she bought from Dr. Mott.

The court record does not record the reaction of people in the courtroom, but it's safe to say that her testimony about the arsenic must have caused some sideways glances. Delphi was once again called to the stand and testified that she never saw any rats at the Lloyd house. Although she said she saw mice every now and then, she never saw any rats and doubted the house ever had any.

"Ain't any here. Mrs. Lloyd would not get arsenic without letting me know it," she told the court. "She talked of it but never did get it."

When Delphi was done, the jury deliberated for a few moments and determined that a postmortem examination was in order. So one was ordered. Court was adjourned until 6:30 a.m. the next day. When the court assembled shortly after sunrise, Emily Lloyd was called to the stand once more. She said she had purchased her first order of arsenic from Dr. Edwards while living at the other house. Then, she said, she purchased another order from Edwards and lost it. Then she purchased yet another order from Dr. Mott two or three weeks after that.

She said she purchased it for rats and that she did not burn it the same day she brought it home. The most recent arsenic purchase, she said, had been earlier that month—more than a week before the last of her children became ill. Then she told the court that she did not purchase any arsenic between the first sickness of the child on March 11 and her last sickness on March 23, when she died.

Dr. Mott was then recalled to the stand. Once again, he testified that Emily Lloyd had purchased the arsenic from him on March 18, 1872. He even brought the register to show the court the record of the sale. Then, Attwell was recalled to the stand and remembered trying to persuade Emily Lloyd that an examination of her dead child was in order.

"What's the use? The child is dead now," she said, according to Attwell. "All the Lloyd family died the same way."

At this point, the postmortem examination was entered into evidence, and Dr. Mott was once again called to the stand. He said he found the child's omentum and duodenum very much engorged, although he added that the stomach seemed free from inflammation while the lungs and liver were normal. One of the jurors then asked about the stomach, and the doctor replied that it did not show signs of congestion, although Mott concluded that he believed the child died of congestion of the stomach.

Then Dr. Cross was called back to the stand, testifying that he had seen nothing in his examination to make him think the girl had sufficient inflammation or engorgement to cause death. But he added that it was possible that the blood might have passed in the moments before death, leaving the stomach in a state that showed no inflammation. Even so, there might have been enough inflammation that it could have seemed as though it were the cause of death.

The stomach was then placed in a glass jar, sealed and delivered to Coroner Robert Bentley. He was supposed to deliver it to Professor William Tonery in Baltimore for analysis, although his possession of the evidence was later questioned in court. For now, though, members of the jury were asked to adjourn until the coroner called them back.

"For nearly three weeks, our people were held in a state of feverish excitement awaiting the result of the analysis," the *Mirror* reported.

Then it happened. It was a Saturday. The jury was reassembled in a secret session. There, in the hushed silence of the courthouse, a telegraph from

Professor Tonery was read aloud. It was announced to members of the jury that he had found a grain and a half of arsenic in the stomach. Drs. Mott, Cross and Edwards were summoned to the courthouse at once and asked what was considered a usual dose of arsenic. All three of the doctors concurred that anything more than a tenth of a grain would be deadly.

It didn't take long before members of the jury issued an indictment. Within moments, a warrant was issued for the arrest of Emily Lloyd. She was placed in the custody of Sergeant Attwell.

"The news of this action spread like wildfire," the *Mirror* reported, "and the most intense excitement prevailed."

By the time the carriage containing Emily Lloyd arrived in front of the mayor's office, the street was almost completely blockaded. Now the job of the coroner was done, and he could step aside. Management of the case was handed over to Justice James Wallace.

Shortly after 9:30 a.m., Emily Lloyd entered the mayor's office escorted by Sergeant Attwell. The *Mirror* reported that she was dressed in black and seemed "a little pale."

"She was much more composed than might be expected, though; in the course of the proceedings, once or twice she was deeply affected and moved to tears."

Harrison and Foster appeared as her lawyers. Charles Lee was on hand as the prosecuting attorney. A hush fell over the courtroom as Harrison asked the court that Emily Lloyd be admitted to bail on the grounds that no testimony presented so far in court could justify commitment. The judge determined that she should be held to bail in the sum of $2,000 for her appearance at 10:00 a.m. the next day. Samuel Orrison, the guardian of the children, became her bondsman and declared his intention

"He is a solid member of this community, and a bluff, good-natured, intelligent Virginian who believes firmly in the innocence of the accused," wrote a visiting correspondent from the *New York Herald*.

The crowd dispersed. The accused was driven home. The *Mirror* described her countenance as solid:

> *From the commencement of the investigation to ascertain the cause of death of Maud down to the present hour, she has been cool, calm and collected—asserting all the time in the most insinuating manner, her entire innocence, evincing the most perfect confidence that a thorough investigation will only result in her vindication, a confidence which neither the astounding revelation from Prof. Tonery, nor the trying ordeal of Saturday night appear*

to have shaken in the slightest degree. On Monday, she was engaged in her usual household duties, planning and arranging for the future, with as much composure as if she was not already held by the strong arm of the law, to answer a charge the most revolting of which the human mind can conceive, God grant that her faith is well founded and that she need fear no danger.

At precisely ten o'clock the next morning, the courthouse bell began to ring. A crowd of eager spectators had already assembled that chilly April morning to witness the proceedings. Emily Lloyd arrived dressed in black and on the arm of George Nixon, a retired farmer in his eighties. She took her seat near the stove. At 11:30 a.m., Coroner Bentley walked into the crowded courtroom and delivered the official report from Professor Tonery:

RESULTS OF ANALYSIS

Sample: A stomach and contents; received March 27th, 1872—from Recorder R.M. Bentley of Leesburg, Va. with instructions to determine the absence of presence of arsenic in the contents. I have examined the contents of the above mentioned stomach, which I find to contain about a grain and half poison of Arsenic (arsenous acid)

W.P. TONERY
Analytical Chemist

A hush fell over the court. This was it—the smoking gun, incontrovertible evidence that Emily Lloyd had poisoned her own daughter with arsenic. The accused woman leaned her head on the back of the chair and seemed, as the *Mirror* reported, "deeply affected." The judge heard arguments from both sides and then refused to grant bail. Emily was sent to jail to await the action of the grand jury, which was scheduled to meet the second Monday in June.

"She heard the decision of the court with apparent composure," the *Mirror* reported. "A carriage was ordered, and in charge of the proper officers she was conveyed to jail, where, within the gloomy walls of her prison cell, we must, for the present, leave her."

The *Mirror* didn't leave her for long. The next week, the newspaper published yet another dispatch about the Leesburg scandal that had all the tongues wagging. Apparently, the day after Emily Lloyd was sent to jail, the commonwealth's attorney and the sheriff went to Union Cemetery and oversaw the disinterment of the other dead family members.

"There lay the hastily arranged lot," the newspaper reported.

> *Side by side lay the father and the two little boys—beautiful tombstones marking the spots of their last repose—and the green grass of early spring spreading, like a mantle of velvet, over their peaceful graves, while at their feet, the fresh turned earth of two little mounds, spoke more plainly than words could utter, the untimely taking off of ANNIE and of MAUD.*

A group of curious spectators gathered in the graveyard to witness the macabre spectacle. A solemn stillness hung in the air. The smell of death was overwhelming. Henry Lloyd was the first body to be uncovered. But when the lid of the coffin was removed, Drs. Mott and Cross discovered that the body was so far decomposed and covered with the mosses of death that very little remained but the skeleton frame, which had already started to crumble. So the lid was replaced, and the coffin was lowered once more.

And then Henry Lloyd was returned to his eternal slumber there in Union Cemetery, where he remains today. The doctors then decided that the remains of George Lloyd should not be disturbed, so they turned their attention to Annie Lloyd. The coffin was raised, and the lid was opened. Inside the casket, doctors discovered the child-sized corpse—still relatively

Detail of the headstone for Henry Lloyd and George Lloyd. *Photo by Michael Lee Pope.*

lifelike after two months underground. Her clothes were still bright and perfect, down to the white ribbon holding back her golden curls. She was still wearing bracelets on her arms and a golden chain around her neck, which sparkled in the sunlight after spending months in a cold, dark grave. The doctors dissected the stomach and liver, sealing the organs in a glass jar, which was sent to Professor Tonery in Baltimore.

Meanwhile, Emily Lloyd was imprisoned in a cell on the first floor of the jail. The *Mirror* reported that she was "perfectly resigned to her imprisonment." Her cell was well furnished with her own furniture, and several pictures hung on the wall. She even had two or three flowers growing in the window, relieving the room of its forbidding air of gloom. Visitors said she seemed cheerful, calmly chatting with guests. She even spoke warmly of the treatment she was receiving, adding that she had no desire to be bailed.

If she were released on bail, she explained to anyone who would listen, she would stay at her house. She would essentially be a prisoner at her house anyway, so it made little difference whether she was in jail or at home. At least she had the company of her jailers while incarcerated. And in her house, she would have to hear the hushed whispers of disapproval from her neighbors. Even so, the Victorian sense of propriety was evident in the period dispatches from the *Mirror*:

> *The circumstances attending the entire transaction have woven a dark cloud that now rests with portentous fury over her head. Yet it is possible that the penetrating eye of the law may peer through the accumulated mists, and in so doing purify the moral atmosphere of the taint that rendered investigation a necessity. Until then, let us not judge too harshly, but endeavor to exercise the unfortunate* woman*—who, even if guilty, we are bound to pity—those cardinal virtues "Faith, Hope and Charity."*

Meanwhile, the Lloyd house was shuttered and empty. A correspondent from the *New York Herald* described the scene as morbid. Between two lamps on a black mantelpiece, over the fireplace, an old-fashioned clock had ceased to pace the steps of time. Trinkets were strewn about the parlor, arranged on mantles and tables, even though the house was empty of children. The faces of the four dead children haunted the house in large and nicely framed pictures hung along the walls. Squares of quilt were in a basket on the sofa, the handiwork of a mother abandoned when her last remaining child slipped away.

"There are so many terrible, untrue stories told that I feel glad to be able to have them set right," Emily Lloyd told the correspondent from the *Herald*. "And I know that you will do justice."

"Yes," the Yankee journalist told the southern woman. "I shall be glad to state fairly whatever you may desire to give me for that purpose."

Emily began by recounting the death of her husband, Charles Lloyd, four years earlier. She said he had been sick some time with pneumonia and that on the day he died, he had seemed better that morning. So about 7:00 a.m. or so, he asked for a roasted apple. Emily Lloyd said that she immediately sent to a local restaurant for some apples and that she set out to roast them as soon as they arrived. When they were ready, her ailing husband asked his doting wife to take the rind off and core the apple out before mixing it with some currant jelly. She told the New York journalist that she did so as he sat up in bed near her.

When the apples were ready, he ate them. Then he received some visitors. When the last man left, Charles Lloyd said he was feeling much better. Just then, she said, he dropped back and died suddenly.

"Everyone who knew him knew that he had been long a sufferer with misery in his right breast," she said.

Next up was Mrs. Hammerly of Washington, Emily Lloyd's elderly aunt. People in Leesburg had been quietly whispering that Emily Lloyd was also responsible for the death of this woman, which the accused vehemently denied to her interviewer. She said she took the best possible care of her aunt during her illness, even neglecting her own children in the process.

"I did for her all that it was possible for one human being to do for another," she said. "Yet I am accused of killing her."

Next, she moved on to the deaths of her four children, breaking down in tears several times during the interview. After the death of her husband, she said, she lived for her children. Now that she was a widow and facing a life of raising two boys and two girls by herself, Emily Lloyd explained, she invested every amount of attention she could into them.

"They were smart, bright children, and I set great store upon them," she said. "I often denied myself for them and took great pleasure in doing so."

George and Henry had never been blackberry picking, she explained, before that July morning in 1870 when they went out to enjoy the wild fruit. She explained that they came back before the sun was hot, about 9:00 a.m. By nightfall, she said, they had broken out around the hands and mouth. The doctor thought it was poison oak, and the boys were sick for nearly two weeks before dying at the end of July. When they were gone, she was left with two young mouths to feed.

"I felt that in my sorrow that I had much yet to live for," she said, "and I was happy doing for them."

Here again, the *Herald* correspondent explained, Emily Lloyd got choked up and began weeping bitterly. For a while, she said through the tears, all went well. She was feeling happy, and the children were healthy—until February, when Annie became ill. She lingered for five long and difficult days and then died.

"But I still had one left," she told the journalist, "and contended myself with doing the best for the dead and caring for my living child."

Maud was a beautiful girl, although her mother said the girl "could not talk plain." She could, however, recite Bible verses and hymns. By the end of March, the last remaining child became ill. Within two days, she was dead. Emily Lloyd described herself as disconsolate with grief.

"When I lost her I felt that I had nothing more to live for," she said. "I have no relatives here, and although the members of my church are very kind and come to see me, I feel that I am now alone in the world."

She told the journalist that it was hard to be suspected of doing "such horrid things." But she also told him that she could feel confident that God knew she was innocent. He asked if she suspected that her servant Delphi might have been the cause of the family's trouble. Emily Lloyd immediately responded no, she did not think the African American woman was responsible for the health problems of her husband and children.

The reporter then asked to meet Delphi, whom he described as "a bright mulatto girl, apparently about twenty years of age." She described Emily Lloyd, whom she called "Miss Em," as a mother to her, adding that she would rather die than see her get into any kind of trouble.

The trial began at 10:00 a.m. on Wednesday, October 23, 1872, with Judge James Keith on the bench. Mortimer Kilgour and John Orr were at the prosecutor's table. Eppa Hunton, P. Harrison and J.W. Foster represented the defense. The accused was led into the courtroom on the arm of William Nixon and took her seat in the prisoner's box. She was dressed in black, looking pale and thin. The clerk read the indictment.

"Not guilty," she replied.

Dozens of men were called to the courthouse as potential jurors, all of whom were interviewed. The *Mirror* reported that "the excuses offered by the veniremen were varied, and some were amusing." Sixteen jurors were eventually selected by prosecutors, and the defense had the opportunity to reject four. By that time, it was late in the evening, and the court was about to adjourn. The judge decided against swearing them in at that hour,

Leesburg Courthouse. *Courtesy of the Ethel Littlejohn Adams Photographic Collection, Thomas Balch Library.*

although he sternly instructed them against conducting any conversations about the case. Court adjourned at 10:00 p.m.

The next morning, court convened at the appointed hour with the prisoner in her box. The indictment was read once again, charging Emily Lloyd with causing the death of her daughter on March 25, 1872, by the administration of white arsenic. At that point, commonwealth's attorney Mortimer Kilgour rose and opened the case for the prosecution. The prosecutor warned jurors that a "high and important" duty was ahead of them:

> *That the charge of murder against a human being was terrible under any circumstances—thrilling every nerve, and in the contemplation of which the stoutest heart shrinks. But that murder by a woman, that sex toward whom, in our chivalric devotion we are ever ready to render homage, and whose very weakness appeals to all high-minded men for protection and that woman, as in this case, a mother—the murderer of her own child, the offspring of her own bosom, was doubly appalling. The sweetest words in the english language were mother, home and Heaven. Mother first, because*

> *at its very mention all the tenderest sympathies of our nature gush forth, and memories turn to the days of childhood, when bending at the maternal knee, the holiest altar known to man, we first lisped our "Our Father who art in heaven." When we remember that it was from this altar, with all the maternal affections dried up, and its little hands hypocritically clasped in her own, the unnatural mother dragged her child not to dash out its brains in the fury and heat of passion, but to rob it of life by the insidious means of poison, we can comprehend in all its far reaching solemnity, the duty this day devolves upon us. And in trying the case, they were not to know woman, mother, friends or relatives—and if the verdict consigned Mrs. Lloyd to the gallows tree or remanded her back to the desolated hearthstone that would no longer be cheered by the innocent prattle of her children, be it so they were the mere ministers of the law to execute its mandates.*

Attorney James William Foster rose to offer the defense, criticizing the manner in which prosecutors were managing the case against Emily Lloyd and the secrecy that preceded the trial. He warned members of the jury that they should not be "beguiled" by the eloquence of counsel. He compared the suspicions of guilt to the "cloud Elijah witnessed," a reference to the first book of Kings in which Elijah was sent to confront King Ahab of Israel and his wicked wife, Jezebel, on Mount Carmel.

Emily Lloyd became the Jezebel of Leesburg, a woman whose infamy became the stuff of legend. Like the cloud that Elijah witnessed, this scandal gathered on the horizon and transformed the sky into a dark tapestry of intrigue. This Jezebel had been around the block, apparently. Just after the clerk swore in the witnesses, the prosecutor informed the court that one of the jurors had admitted that Emily Lloyd had been "a sweetheart" of his and that he wouldn't consent to do anything with her even if she had "poisoned a hundred people." The *Mirror* did not report what happened to the juror, although the revelation must have been shocking to the Victorian sensibilities of the era.

The first witness called to the stand was Delphi Lazenburg, the servant girl employed in the Lloyd house for many years. She recounted the story of how Maud had taken sick on a Saturday and died the following Monday. The African American woman testified about how Maud "threw up a good deal" and appeared to have a fever. When she complained of "a hurting in the stomach," the doctor gave her limewater and milk. Delphi told the court she was in the habit of cleaning up the place, so she threw out the vomit—not knowing that it could potentially become a key piece

Detail of headstone for Annie Lloyd and Maud Lloyd *Photo by Michael Lee Pope.*

of evidence in a murder trial. When she was asked about arsenic, Delphi testified that that she knew nothing about the purchase of the substance. She said she never saw any rats or any rat holes, adding that she saw some mice but never saw any poison.

At this point, members of the jury were sent away from the courtroom so the lawyers could make arguments to the judge about whether to admit testimony calculated to implicate Emily Lloyd in the deaths of her other children, deaths that were not included in the charges against her. The defense attorney objected to its introduction, citing several legal issues. Then the prosecutor had his turn, arguing that it was important to show the connection between Maud's death and those of the other children. The court reserved its decision, and Delphi was called back to the stand. She had little to add to the conversation, however, other than that she had never smelled anything unusual burning.

Dr. Mott was then called to the stand. He testified that he had been a physician since 1865, and he had known the prisoner for thirty years. He explained that he had attended to Maud in her last illness and found her suffering and complaining of problems in her bowels. He gave her calomel and opium. When he saw her the next day, he testified, she seemed better. He gave her bismuth and opium with limewater and milk. And yet by the time he arrived along with Dr. Cross for a visit the next morning, she had deteriorated once again.

She died about noon, he explained to the jury with clinical detachment.

Maud passed from this earth quietly, he explained, and she bore no unusual signs. Then he testified about the postmortem examination, detailing how he had prepared the stomach in a glass jar. He explained how he sealed it and gave it to Coroner Bentley to be carried to Professor Tonery for analysis. Dr. Mott told the jury that it was his decided opinion that Maud did not die of "arsenical poisoning," although he added that he had never actually seen a death from this cause. He told the jury he had concluded that the cause of death was congestion of the stomach, although the postmortem examination showed no evidence of such.

By the time Dr. Mott concluded his testimony, the hour of 6:00 p.m. had arrived, so the judge determined court concluded for the day. Jurors were instructed not to discuss the case—although the case was so sensational that one can imagine the conversations that must have taken place around the hearthstones of Leesburg on that cold October evening.

Court convened at 10:00 a.m. the next day, and the judge promptly ruled against the admissibility of evidence connecting Emily Lloyd to the deaths of her other children. This was a crushing blow for the prosecution, which could have used the power of multiplication to convict the prisoner. Even if the evidence had been weak, the accumulation of details could have been overwhelming for members of the jury. Instead, the case was now focused solely on the death of little Maud.

Delphi was once again called to the stand. She returned to the events of Saturday, March 23, when Maud was first taken sick. The servant girl explained how she had purchased a cake from Mrs. Green's bakery. Maud ate the cake, Delphi testified, and immediately began vomiting. The poor dying child ate nothing at all on Sunday, she explained. But on cross-examination, the defense attorney reminded her that she had previously testified that the child had eaten pot roast, tea and toast on Sunday.

Delphi responded that she had forgotten about that, scoring a point for the defense team trying to undercut testimony that might incriminate their client.

On further cross-examination, Delphi testified that she had seen one dead mouse in the passage of the house and a live rat in the yard after Maud's death. When the defense attorney asked her if she had spoken to anybody about what she would say in court, she acknowledged that she had spoken to the prosecutors about her testimony but had been instructed to tell the truth without regard to who would be harmed. She ended with a tearful account of how she and Emily Lloyd had been "much affected" by the death of the girl.

John Orr, one of the prosecutors, then took the stand and explained that Delphi had, in fact, been to his office. He acknowledged that he had wanted to know what her testimony would be, although he added that he warned her to speak the truth, whatever it might be. Prosecutors then called James Wallace, one of the justices, to recount the testimony of Coroner Robert Bentley, who had recently died. He explained how the coroner was on the record about how he had transported the glass jar containing Maud's stomach to Professor Tonery to make the all-important analysis of its contents.

The defense attorney leapt to his feet and objected to the introduction of testimony from a dead man. As he had done before, the judged decided that he would defer a decision until later and then ordered the court to proceed with its business. Once again, one of the most important decisions in the case was held in limbo while both sides held their breaths and spectators wondered what would happen next.

At this point, Dr. Cross was called to the stand. He said he had been a doctor in Leesburg for thirty-five years and that he had been with Dr. Mott on that March day when they visited Maud at the Lloyd house and found her in *articulo mortis*, essentially at the point of death. He recommended a hot bath and a hot toddy and then left a prescription of morphine, cerium and Huxham's tincture of bark. He told the court he did not stay more than five minutes, though, because he believed that the girl would die within fifteen minutes.

"The pupils of the eyes were greatly dilated, showing great irritation of the brain," the doctor told jurors. "The cheeks were tumefied and the patient was in a comatose state, indicating complete exhaustion."

Dr. Cross acknowledged that he had never seen a case of poisoning by arsenic, although this one fit all the hallmarks from his reading about the subject. But he warned that a number of diseases, such as cholera or cholera morbus, would produce the same symptoms of violent vomiting and purging. This case, though, was different, he told the court. He suspected at the time that the death had been produced by "some unnatural cause."

"But no man could pretend to determine the presence of poison in the stomach without analyzing it," the doctor testified.

He told the jury that he thought half a grain of arsenic was sufficient to kill a child of three or four years old. The substance would not remain in the stomach inert, though. The doctor then explained to the court how arsenic would be absorbed by the liver or thrown out by the urinary organs. This would take from a half hour to two hours after being taken into the stomach, according to the doctor's testimony.

Court then adjourned for the day. Jurors must have been struggling to process everything they had heard up to that point—a steady stream of conflicting information and contradictory impulses. As night fell that evening and members of the jury returned home, a sense of uncertainty hung over the strange trial of Emily Lloyd.

The next morning began with Dr. Cross being called to the stand once more. He explained that he had taken part in the postmortem examination with Dr. Mott. He explained how the jar with the stomach was given to Bentley to be conveyed to Tonery. He told the jurors how Emily Lloyd had stated positively that she had purchased no arsenic between the time of Annie's death, which occurred in February, and Maud's death, on March 25.

Dr. Cross also testified that he had been present with Professor Tonery when Maud's body was exhumed, as well as when it was examined by Professor Louis Tiffany two months later. The doctor said he was there when the professor removed certain portions of the intestines and sealed them in a jar. He said it was the same body on which he made his postmortem examination and that he recognized it from the absence of the stomach and the presence of the silk he used in the postmortem. On cross-examination, Dr. Cross went into detail about the symptoms of arsenical poison.

Next on the stand was a surprise witness, Magdalene Green, someone who had known the prisoner for years. In shocking testimony, she told the court that Emily Lloyd had stopped by her house the previous January and asked to buy some arsenic. A hush must have fallen over the courtroom at that point. Here was a piece of evidence that might show that Emily Lloyd had been on the hunt for the poison for some time—an indication of premeditation.

The witness said the accused had some story about rats, although it seems unlikely that story carried much weight with Green. She told the court she had refused to comply with the request—and that Emily Lloyd responded by running off and getting it herself. Green said she knew this because the prisoner called again on her way back and offered to give the witness some of it. Emily Lloyd later said that she "lost" the arsenic on her way home. Green said that she knew nothing of Maud's sickness until she heard the girl was dead.

That opened the floodgates. The next witness was Julian Hutchson, who said that he had sold Emily Lloyd an ounce of arsenic in April 1870. Jurors now had a clear indication that the accused had access to arsenic, at least if they were willing to believe the witnesses. And the defense attorneys did little to counteract their credibility.

But that wasn't all.

Mollie Ryon was next on the stand. She said she was at the Lloyd house the Sunday before the girl died and that she saw the child sitting up and

The drugstore where Emily Lloyd purchased arsenic. *Courtesy of the Ethel Littlejohn Adams Photographic Collection, Thomas Balch Library.*

playing on the lounge. The woman testified that she did not see the child eat or drink anything while she was there, although she did hear rats in the house during the night when she sat up with Maud. Ryon testified that the accused seemed as fond of Maud as mothers generally are of their children.

A series of witnesses was then called to the stand who knew Emily Lloyd, detailing events leading up to her daughter's death—how the mother was dutifully looking after her daughter, how she gave her a bath in the hours before her death, how friends and relatives knew nothing about the girl's sickness. Matthew Ball rounded out the testimony for the day, telling members of the jury that he had been a clerk at Mott & Metzger's drugstore the day Emily came in to purchase half an ounce of arsenic.

Poison was also on the menu when prosecutors called Jason Head to the stand. Head, who was a next-door neighbor in Leesburg, told the jury about how his chickens had mysteriously died in late March. He said he was sick at the time and wasn't sure what happened to them. Prosecutors were clearly trying to build a case that the fowl had eaten the vomit thrown up by Maud, which caused their death.

Town sergeant Bernard Attwell was next on the stand. He told the court how Samuel Orrison went to visit Emily Lloyd after Maud's death. He explained how he had recommended a postmortem examination and how she had initially refused but finally consented. After that, he said, he made arrangements for the inquest and then returned to let Emily Lloyd know what was to be done and when. He found her in bed. She asked him to come close.

"You remember the old rascal I was talking to you about last night?" she asked.

"No," he replied.

She said it was Bill Lloyd, brother of her dead husband—a man who was no friend. She said if harm had come to the children, it would be through "the instrumentality" of Bill Lloyd and Pat Gill. She explained how she had gotten milk and butter from Gill that morning. Delphi reminded her that all of the family had partaken of the milk, and it did not make them all sick.

Attwell then recalled the postmortem, explaining how after the stomach had been taken from the body, it was wrapped in a white cloth and taken to Dr. Mott's office, where it was placed on the counter until a bottle was washed and cleaned to receive it. The witness left the stand and then returned in dramatic fashion to clarify an important point: the stomach was placed in a glass jar at the house and then carried to the drugstore.

His memory was faulty, he explained, adding that it had been refreshed after he left the stand. Undoubtedly, prosecutors buttonholed him in the cramped courthouse and demanded that he correct the record. They might have been afraid that the defense would have a field day poking holes in the scientific voracity of the case against Emily Lloyd by questioning what happened to Maud's stomach after it was taken from her body, who had possession of it and whether it had been corrupted in the process. Here we see the first evidence that prosecutors understood this could be a fatal weakness of their prosecution.

The next few witnesses detailed the mechanics of exhuming the body and collecting forensic evidence. The undertaker testified that the doctor sprinkled some kind of lime on the girl before using his knife in the cemetery. The gravedigger told jurors he also saw the doctor sprinkle something over the body before using the knife. Dry goods merchant Henry Claggett told jurors that he was present for the postmortem and that he saw the stomach placed into a black bottle before being given to Bentley.

John Drish was next on the stand, testifying that he was in Mott & Metzger's drugstore the night of the postmortem examination, when Bentley walked in with the girl's stomach in a glass jar. He said the jar was sealed in his presence, adding that Dr. Mott washed off the outside of the bottle and returned it to Bentley. At this point, Henry Claggett was called back to the stand to clarify that the bottle was sealed with beeswax.

The prosecution said the next witness it would call would be Professor Tonery. But there was a problem. The witness would need daylight to make a presentation about his analysis. And because it was almost 6:00 p.m. on a winter afternoon, the courtroom was too dark. So the judge adjourned the trial until the next day.

The sun was shining brightly the next morning, a Saturday. It was a stark contrast to the dark and rainy weather of the previous few days—undoubtedly a welcome change for members of the jury, who were stuck in court. Inside the courtroom, however, the gruesome details of the most sensational murder trial to ever be conducted in Leesburg dragged on. The prosecutor informed the court that the case had now reached the point at which he would be laying the foundation for the analysis of the stomach and other portions of the intestines.

To that end, Professor Louis Tiffany of Baltimore was called to the stand. As a demonstrator of anatomy at Maryland University and a surgeon at Baltimore Hospital, Tiffany was certified by the court as an expert. The professor had come to Leesburg back in May for the purpose of examining several bodies, which he did in the presence of Professor Tonery, as well as Dr. Cross, Dr. Mott, Major Orr and Loudoun sheriff

The Lloyd family plot at Union Cemetery. *Photo by Michael Lee Pope.*

William Barrett. The examination was performed in Union Cemetery, where the body was exhumed.

Tiffany described the appearance of the body, all the way down to the plate on the coffin marked "Maud Lloyd." He said he found it considerably decomposed and offensive. To counteract the odor, he sprinkled lime on the body, although he added that he was careful not to use it on the places where he inserted the knife. In cutting the belly, he said, he found the stomach and portions of the intestines waning.

He also testified that he saw two stomachs in separate jars at the office of Professor Tonery on April 25. One was a small stomach with a small piece of gut attached—the stomach of a child. He said he took from Maud's body the liver, spleen, two kidneys and a portion of large gut. He detailed how he put them in a jar that had been prepared specifically for them and then sealed them and placed labels on them before giving them to Professor Tonery.

At this point, the judge intervened to inform the prosecutors that there was no getting around the fact that they had better be able to prove—with testimony from a living witness—that Maud's stomach had been in the possession of Coroner Robert Bentley from the time it was placed in his charge to the moment it was delivered into the hands of Professor Tonery. Otherwise, the judge said, he could not allow them to introduce the analysis as evidence.

Prosecutors argued that Bentley was a fine and upstanding man, someone who could be trusted with responsibility. His character was unquestioned, they explained, and he had faithfully guarded the stomach all the way to Baltimore. They recounted how the stomach was delivered to Professor Tonery. But the judge wasn't having any of it. After the arguments were over, he ruled that the analysis of the stomach was out.

The prosecution was now stripped bare. It was as if Maud had never been exhumed at all. The prosecutors were suddenly left with no case at all.

But the trial limped forward anyway. The judge ruled that the portions of the body taken by Professor Tonery would be admissible, including the liver, kidneys and spleen. Professor Tonery was called to the stand for another five hours of testimony, beginning with an account of his visit to Leesburg in May with Professor Tiffany. Tonery recounted the exhumation of Maud Lloyd and how the liver, spleen and kidneys were placed in a jar and taken to Baltimore. He testified how he had attached the plate taken from the coffin, marked "Maud Lloyd," as well as how he had scratched the name Maud on the glass.

Furthermore, he added, the jar was never out of his possession except for a few minutes while he was at dinner. Even then, the jar was locked in his room at the hotel, with the key secured in his pocket. When he reached Baltimore, he told the court, the jar was safely secured in his laboratory. He described how the bottle was sealed and how the seal was not broken until he was ready to use the contents.

At this point, the jar was exhibited in the courtroom. One can only imagine the thoughts that must have entered the minds of those assembled in the Loudoun County Courthouse that day as the jar that once held the organs of Maud Lloyd was presented as evidence during her mother's trial. The professor then went on to describe the manner in which he analyzed the liver, spleen and kidneys.

"We took down the professor's analysis," the *Mirror* noted. "But for want of space, we omit it."

The professor's analysis might be lost to history, but what happened next was not. Tonery entered into a discussion of the process he used to remove parts of the body taken from Maud's coffin. The *Mirror* described the testimony as "exceedingly clear and interesting." Step by step, the professor went through the gruesome process. Every piece of equipment he used was new; he explained how he subjected the instruments to several tests before using them. Ultimately, he concluded, he left "no range of possibility for doubting the correctness" of his analysis.

Then it was time for cross-examination. When the defense attorney questioned him, the professor acknowledged that arsenic was sometimes found in bismuth. Then the professor admitted that the quantity was so small that the results could have been from a number of other sources. The defense called Dr. Mott, who testified that that he gave Maud three or four doses from a jar of bismuth. Now the defense was sewing the seeds of doubt, presenting evidence that the doctors might have introduced enough arsenic in Maud to have killed her.

Next on the stand was Theodore Wormly, a professor of chemistry from Columbus, Ohio, who had written a book titled *Micro-Chemistry of Poisons*. Wormly had been a professor since 1852 and spent the last decade studying poisons. He explained that he had never investigated a case of poisoning by arsenic, although he had analyzed about a dozen or so bodies of people who had died as a result of poison. He said that he had heard the testimony of Professor Tonery, adding that he believed that the method and process used for the recovery of poison was proper and that the result must have been arsenic.

Professor Wormly explained that arsenic found is the stomach is inert, adding that death is the result of arsenic being absorbed into the liver. Elimination of arsenic from the stomach, he added, usually happened a few hours after consumption. So when the liver and spleen absorbed some of the arsenic, a larger quantity had been taken in by the stomach. The professor explained that symptoms of poisoning by arsenic could present themselves all at once. Sometimes, they could appear immediately after eating the substance, while other times, they could be delayed as long as sixteen hours.

Next on the stand was legendary professor John William Mallett, analytic chemist for the University of Virginia. He told the court that the testimony offered by Professor Tonery was "fair and clear" and that there was no doubt that arsenic was found. Mallett explained that when he was a student in Germany, he had witnessed one death that was attributed to arsenic and assisted in the analysis after death. Then he went into detail about the various symptoms of poisoning by arsenic. He concluded his testimony by explaining that the carbonate of lime used by Professor Tonery would not have affected the analysis.

By the time Mallet was finished, the clock had struck 6:00 p.m., so court was adjourned for the evening. The next morning, the prisoner was in her box by 10:00 a.m. Dr. Richard Edwards was next on the stand. He detailed

"The Age of Drugs," a 1900 cartoon published in *Puck* magazine. *Courtesy of the Library of Congress.*

PRESCRIPTIONS
CAREFULLY
COMPOUNDED.
STRYCHNINE
ANTIPYRIN
NERVE
STIMULANT
OPIUM
COCAINE
ARSENIC
THE NEEDLE
SOOTHING
SYRUP
Dalrymple

how he had sold half an ounce of arsenic to Emily Lloyd back in March, adding yet another critical detail to the prosecution's theory.

Professor Tiffany was next, repeating his testimony from the previous Saturday, when he had described the appearance of Maud the day she was exhumed and the method he used for dissection. During the examination, he discovered discoloration in the intestines. The professor concluded that the marks could have been natural or unnatural, although he was unable to determine the cause and manner of death because the body had been dead so long.

Professor Tiffany then acknowledged a series of facts in an effort to establish the case against Emily Lloyd: that eighty-six to one hundred grains of arsenic were found in Maud's body, that the symptoms were consistent with poisoning by arsenic and that the body exhibited the anatomical appearance of poisoning by arsenic. The result, the professor offered, could be nothing other than a conclusion that Maud Lloyd was sent to her grave by arsenic.

Samuel Orrison, guardian of the children, was next on the stand to testify about what kind of property was owned by the family. He told the court that the property of the children consisted of two houses valued at $1,500. He also described Emily Lloyd as a "kind and devoted mother," judging from the care she seemed to bestow on the children. Prosecutors closed their case by recalling Professor Wormly, who was asked to reiterate some of the statements in his book on poison.

Now the prosecution had concluded its case—although without its key piece of evidence: Maud's stomach. The defense opened its case, ready to portray Emily Lloyd as an innocent woman caught up in tragic circumstances. Or, at the very least, it was eager to sow enough reasonable doubt to prevent a conviction.

First on the stand for the defense was Dr. Gruliam Ellzey, a graduate of the Department of Analytical Chemistry at the University of New York. The defense team began by establishing him as an expert who paid particular attention to the subject of chemistry in his practice as a physician. He testified that the process Professor Tonery used to analyze the liver, kidney and spleen was a correct one, although he added that it was not "precisely accurate" in separating the arsenical compounds from other compounds. He testified that he was not satisfied that the matters he weighed were free of moisture, and he added that he believed the prosecution witness failed to prove that the substances had been dry when they were weighed.

Dr. William Taylor of Richmond then took the stand to administer some more tough medicine for the government's case. On the stand, he said he had seen seven or eight cases of poisoning by arsenic, and he had analyzed even more stomachs of people who had succumbed to the substance. He agreed with Ellzey that the system of weights and measurements was flawed, adding to the doubt that jurors were now having about the elaborate case prosecutors had spent days outlining. He explained that the symptoms of poisoning by arsenic were so varied that it was often difficult to determine whether it was a cause at all. He said the exact same symptoms could be produced by many other causes.

The chorus of doubt continued as Dr. P.B. Wilson of Baltimore took the stand. Although he said he agreed with the "manipulations" of Professor Tonery, he described the manner of weighing as "undetermined." On the witness stand, Wilson also said Tonery did not use sufficient precaution in drying. He also said he would never have allowed the use of carbonate of lime unless he could be absolutely sure it was pure.

At that point, it was 5:00 p.m., and the judge determined it was time to adjourn. When court gaveled into session the next day at 10:00 a.m., a considerably smaller crowd had assembled. The first agenda item of the day was whether the court should admit Dr. Ellzey's analysis of the bismuth. He told the jurors that he conducted five separate analyses of bismuth, and he exhibited the results of the last one to the jury in metallic spots on a china cup. He said that he was pretty sure that the child died of arsenic poisoning, although he would be "more cautious" in court on the stand.

While jurors were trying to pay attention to the medical details about how human organs are probed and prodded by doctors, many of them probably turned their attention to Emily Lloyd. There, in the prisoner's box, she occupied her seat with a kind of stoicism. Although she was seen to laugh every now and then when the lawyers made witty remarks, for the most part, she remained stone cold serious throughout the trail. Nobody in court seemed to be her friend, even the lawyers who surrounded her. Sometimes she would read a newspaper furnished by the correspondent from the *Alexandria Gazette*. She seemed to chat with the sheriff more than her own lawyers. The *Mirror* described her as "apparently as unconcerned as the most listless spectator."

> *If innocent of the fearful crime with which she stands charged, who can fathom the mental agony she has endured during the past week? If guilty her stoicism is unaccountable, and stamps her the most heartless of criminals. The story of how the body of her dead child was taken from the grave—its vital parts removed to a distant city, and in the dingy laboratory of the*

> *chemist, cut up and cooked as you would a man's dinner was sufficiently harrowing to appall the stoutest heart, had it been solely in the interests of science. But when it is for the purpose of proving* the mother is the murderer, *we involuntarily turn with a shudder from the scene, and await the closing events of the sad drama.*

Opening arguments began on the first day of October, a cold and gray Wednesday morning. John Orr opened the argument for the prosecution. The *Mirror* described his closing argument as "a well-arranged argument of considerable length," although that's the extent of the description. He was followed by Powell Harrison, who argued that the commonwealth had failed to make its case. Harrison said prosecutors were unable to prove that Maud Lloyd was poisoned. He said the chemist who conducted the analysis was either incompetent or corrupt, adding that the body was improperly exhumed. As for the arsenic that might have been found, he said, it could have been accounted for in the carbonate of lime that was sprinkled on the body when it was exhumed. Arsenic might have also been on the dissecting knives. Then there was the alternative theory that the child took poison by accident.

Eppa Hunton continued the closing arguments for the defense. Hunton, a former Confederate general who was wounded in Pickett's Charge at the Battle of Gettysburg, analyzed all the testimony that jurors had heard, going through it witness by witness. The *Mirror* described his comments as "a touching appeal" for "the almost friendless widow" and "childless mother" who was sitting before them in the prisoner's box. The next morning, Matthew Harrison spoke for the defense, and Mortimer Kilgour closed for the government.

"Each did his duty," reported the *Mirror*, "the one to the prisoner and the other to the commonwealth with power of logic and a beauty of eloquence worthy of the best bars in the state."

Now, after eight days of hearing testimony and arguments, members of the jury finally retreated behind closed doors. It was shortly after 5:30 p.m. on a Monday afternoon. History records no witness to what was said by members of the jury, who were finally able to talk about the case to one another for the first time. It didn't take them long.

Twenty minutes: not guilty.

Despite the hours and hours of evidence, members of the jury had already entered their verdict before 6:00 p.m. that afternoon. The judge thanked them for their service and then told them that the court concurred with their decision. A correspondent for the *Baltimore Sun* reported that

Emily Lloyd was observed to "smile frequently," although nobody seemed to approach her to offer congratulations—"not even a relative." Emily Lloyd walked out of the courtroom a free woman on the arm of Sheriff Nixon. The *Mirror* closed the scene on the case this way:

> *Thus closed one of the most remarkable trails ever witnessed in Loudoun—one that has occasioned more excitement among our own people and occupied more excitement among our own people, and occupied a larger space in the public mind than any ever before tried in this county. And here the curtain falls. God grant that we may never be called on to record its like again.*

4

First Contact

Murder and Mayhem in the New World

Settlers and natives clash in the Old Dominion.

The story of European arrival in Northern Virginia is often told through the gauzy nostalgia of John Smith sailing up the Potomac River and greeting the natives. The truth is much more wicked.

It's a story of kidnapping and deception, betrayal and bloodshed, power and domination. And it doesn't end well.

Spanish admiral Menéndez de Avilés was the first European to sail into the Chesapeake Bay, a scene that was so inspiring that he called it the "Bay of the Mother of God." His first attempt to conquer the area in 1566 was a complete flop. But the Spanish were back a few years later in 1570, when a group of Jesuits sailed up the James River and built a chapel, where the Indians killed eight of the nine missionaries. Other Spanish missions met with a similar fate throughout Tidewater Virginia.

The English didn't have better luck.

When Captain Bartholomew Gilbert sailed into the Chesapeake Bay in 1603, the locals opened fire. A few years later, Captain Samuel Mace found a more accommodating tribe when he encountered the Rappahannock. Mace returned the favor by killing the chief and kidnapping several of the tribesmen, who were taken back to England to give dugout demonstrations on the Thames River. This and other European misadventures got the attention of Powhatan, a powerful Indian sachem who ruled a vast confederacy stretching from the chief's headquarters at Werowocomoco

Menéndez de Avilés. *Courtesy of the Library of Congress.*

Pocahontas. *Courtesy of the Library of Congress.*

through Northern Virginia and into Maryland.

The chief refused to sell corn to the settlers when they needed it most. When the English became desperate, Powhatan summoned John Smith to Werowocomoco in December 1607. When Smith arrived, the Indians took him into captivity

"At each place, I expected when they would execute me," Smith would later recall.

Powhatan now held Smith's life in his hands. This is a scene the sachem must have savored for a few moments, the culmination of a life seeking to expand his power and influence. Powhatan's father had been chief of a southern tribe that was driven north by Spanish conquistadors. The experience turned him into a conqueror in his own right, and when Powhatan's father arrived in Virginia, he took control over several local tribes.

The son took over the family business, adding several more Tidewater tribes and creating a confederacy. By the time the English arrived in Northern Virginia, Powhatan had already consolidated his rule and stature. More than two hundred tribes paid taxes and provided military support to Powhatan. These days, Powhatan is probably remembered best for being the father of the beautiful Pocahontas.

But reality was not as saccharine as a Disney picture.

According to Smith's account, two large stones were brought to Powhatan. The tribesmen dragged Smith to the stones, forcing his head down. Then they brought out the clubs, ostensibly to beat out his brains. Pocahontas is said to have saved him by placing her head on his when her father raised his war club to execute him. Some have argued the ritual was intended as a way to induct him into the tribe. Others have charged Smith with lying about the story to gain popularity.

John Smith. *Courtesy of the Library of Congress.*

Years later, Pocahontas came to Northern Virginia to trade goods with the Patawomeck. This tribe, based in Stafford County, is the reason we now call the river leading to Mount Vernon the Potomac. It's also the tribe that sold Powhatan's daughter for a copper kettle. When Captain Samuel Argoll learned that Pocahontas had been with the Patawomeck for three months, he devised a trick to capture her. He offered the chief a kettle if the tribe would induce Pocahontas to board his ship.

As a result of the subterfuge, Pocahontas was kidnapped in 1613. The captain would later explain that he wanted to ransom her for some English prisoners held by Chief Powhatan. Apparently, he also had his eye on weapons and farming tools Powhatan's people had stolen. Nobody was turning swords to plowshares, though. Powhatan returned the prisoners but created a standoff when he declined to turn over enough weapons and tools to satisfy the Patawomeck.

Pocahontas eventually fell in love with an English widower by the name of John Rolfe. So she was baptized in a famous ritual immortalized in a painting that hangs in the Capitol Dome. Then she married Rolfe, a union that is still debated today because it had its roots in kidnapping and deception.

By 1609, the English were ready to declare fealty to Powhatan. So Christopher Newport organized a grand ceremony to declare Chief Powhatan an emperor—as if he needed the additional title. Smith observed that Powhatan seemed to appreciate the gifts more than the title, "he neither knowing the majesty nor meaning of the Crowne." Smith also described the chief as "a tall, well-proportioned man, with a sower [*sic*] look; his head somewhat gray, his beard so thin that it seemeth none at al. His age near 60, of a very able and hardy body."

When Powhatan died in 1618, he tried to leave the succession of power to his brother Opitchapan. But a younger brother, Opechancanough, seized control. In 1622, he led the Powhatans and other Indians on a sneak attack on the Virginia colony that killed more than 350 settlers. Then, in 1644, the old and feeble Opechancanough was captured, and while he was in captivity, a colonist shot him in the back, killing him. This is the wickedness that destroyed the once mighty Powhatan empire.

Take the legend of Simon Kenton, for example. He's Northern Virginia's very own version of Paul Bunyan or Davy Crocket.

Yes, that's right. Northern Virginia has its own infamous pioneer. His legend extends out into the vast expanses of land that were once known as Virginia, places that are now known as Ohio and Kentucky. Stories of his wild youth in Prince William County were once traded late at night over campfires, a legacy that has been preserved for posterity by the dutiful scribes of the Works Progress Administration in the 1930s. That was a time when the legend was still alive and well for a certain population in Northern Virginia.

Simon Kenton was more than six feet tall and had long red hair, a massive man with an oversized personality. He was born on April 3, 1755, in Fauquier County to Mary Miller Kenton and Mark Kenton. The seventh of nine children in a large Irish family from County Down, his family came to Virginia in 1737. They built a cabin near Dumfries at a place called Devil's Bed.

Legend has it that Simon hated working on the farm and preferred roaming and hunting in the woods. Descriptions of him always portray him as robust, even in his youth.

Here was a man who led a fascinating life in a dangerous time. But it was his early history in Virginia that seemed to capture the interest of folklorists, who collected the stories as if they were treasures to be preserved for all time by the Works Progress Administration. When Virginia Workers Project worker Susan Morton collected recollections of Simon Kenton in the 1930s and '40s, the stories were directly proportional to his proximity to the Bull Run Mountains and Fauquier or Prince William Counties.

"Their main topics were the circumstances of his birth, his leaving home, his disguised return, and his half-Indian descendants in the area," wrote Thomas Barden in a 1991 collection of Virginia folk legends. "They also typically gave this extraordinary man an ordinary context."

Reaching back into their memories, these elderly Virginians of an earlier era wove a tale of folk wisdom and sympathetic magic. They portray a man whose future fame was influenced by the folk magic of two elderly women—a kind of supernatural mysticism mixed with frontier toughness. So what made Simon Kenton so extraordinary?

"'Twas most likely th' talk of an old woman what made Simon Kenton th' great man he turned out t' be," said Rebecca Ashby, who was interviewed in the summer of 1941.

When Kenton was born, Ashby explained, he had a dark mole on his neck. According to the folklore of the time, that seemed to be an indication that he would be executed by a hangman's noose. So his mother tried everything she could think of to get rid of the mark.

"She made poultices of herbs an' soaked a coin in vinegar, an' made him wear it over th' mole," Ashby said. "But nothin' ever did any good."

The folklore legend says that his brothers were industrious and successful. One worked with George Washington surveying Northern Virginia. Another became rich as a land speculator. Their success made life difficult for Simon, who was seen as lazy and wild—a boy who excelled only at hunting and tracking. He refused to attend school and remained illiterate all his life.

At the tender age of sixteen, Simon Kenton battled for the attention of a woman with a rival, William Leachman, a man who was much larger and more powerful than the teenager. But Kenton picked a fight and beat Leachman senseless. According to legend, Kenton stepped on a tree.

"It caught on th' other fellow's hair an' pulled him offn' his feet so quick that it took his breath," Ashby explained. "An' then Simon heaved a powerful knock on his chin an' he 'peared t' be dead fer sure."

Believing he had killed Leachman, Kenton set out for parts unknown, assuming the name Simon Butler and joining a hunting expedition to the Ohio River near Fort Pitt. In 1774, Simon fought in a conflict known as Lord Dunmore's War, one that was sparked way out in the part of Virginia that was then known as Kentucky County.

The little-known war began when a group of Delawares, Shawnees and Cherokees captured a group of settlers and tortured them to death. One of the victims was James Boone, the eldest son of an obscure hunter named Daniel Boone. That prompted Virginia governor John Murray, the fourth earl of Dunmore, to ask the House of Burgesses to declare war. Here on the battlefields of Lord Dunmore's War is where Simon Kenton met Daniel Boone, George Rogers Clark and Simon Girty—a group of fierce Indian hunters who would change the direction of his life.

Frontier life was quick and dirty, and perhaps that was part of the wicked appeal for Simon Kenton, who clearly thrived in the environment. During one of the most famous episodes, he saved Boone's life by shooting an Indian who was about to kill him with a tomahawk.

During the Revolutionary War, Kenton served as a scout under George Rogers Clark. At one point early in the war, Kenton was captured by the Shawnees while out on a reconnaissance mission. He was forced to run the gauntlet eight times, and he was lashed to a wild horse that was set free and almost ripped his arm off. He was tied to a stake to be burned alive on three separate occasions, each time culminating in a dramatic rescue. After years of torture and abuse, Kenton was able to escape and returned to Kentucky.

After the Revolutionary War, in 1787, Kenton married Martha Dowden and had four children. Unfortunately, Simon Kenton was frequently away. Such was the case one day in 1796, when the Kenton home burned to the ground. Martha Kenton died as a result of her burns, and a child that would have been their fifth was stillborn.

Two years later, Kenton married Martha's first cousin Elizabeth Jarbo, a woman who was twenty-one years younger than him. She reared five more children for Simon Kenton. In 1799, he moved the family to Springfield, Ohio, where he set up a trading post and gristmill. Even here, he continued battling Indians, including a legendary confrontation with a violent Indian named Bigfoot. Kenton won that fight, too.

Some of his conflicts were not against Indians, though. In 1810, he was served a warrant for being in violation of a debtor's law. Officials tried to put him in the Urbana debtor's prison, but he refused. When friends and associates heard about the conflict, they moved quickly to appoint him sheriff of Urbana.

He died in 1836 and was buried near his cabin at the headwaters of Mad River in Zanesfield, Ohio. He was later reinterred on Kenton Mound at Oak Dale Cemetery in Urbana, where a monument honoring his life stands today.

These days, the name Simon Kenton may be known more widely than the man himself. His name graces a council of the Boy Scouts, an elementary school, a high school, a road and a suspension bridge that connects Ohio and Kentucky. Groups such as the Kanawha Rangers reenact the lifestyles of the long hunters, and documentation of Kenton's presence at a building is often used as an argument for historic preservation.

For some, Simon Kenton's legacy is one of fierce independence and rugged individualism in a time when the young nation was forging its identify. For others, it's an embarrassing narrative of white privilege murdering its way across a native landscape. Whatever the value of Simon Kenton's legacy, it's a story that has its roots planted firmly in wicked Northern Virginia.

5

Tobacco Insurrection

East Versus West in Prince William County

Inspection act prompts armed rebellion.

In the early days of Northern Virginia, the moneyed elite along the Potomac River often clashed with the small farmers who lived inland. The two cultures shared little in common. One group was known as "men of substance," a circle of elite plantation owners who owned large plantations up to the Fall Line. The other group was a motley crew of Scots merchants, ex-convicts and Irish ex-servants. The two groups were often in conflict, sometimes violently.

Such was the case in the part of the commonwealth that would eventually become Prince William County, where some planters gained a reputation for being dishonest businessmen. During the early half of the eighteenth century, many Northern Virginia planters were known to enrich themselves by including inferior tobacco leaves in the hogsheads of tobacco they would ship to London. Some planters would even include the sweepings from their barns.

After a while, purchasing agents took notice, and the price of Virginia tobacco began to fall. This was not acceptable to royal lieutenant governor William Gooch, who ruled in an era when the Virginia governor lived in London and showed little concern for the colony. Gooch, however, did come to Virginia, and he was not about to put up with inferior tobacco. That's why he pushed the Tobacco Inspection Act of 1730, an English law Virginia adopted that was designed to improve the quality of tobacco

Some planters would include sweepings from their barns into their hogsheads of tobacco, enriching themsevles but reducing the quality of the product. *Courtesy of the Library of Congress.*

exported from colonial Virginia. The act mandated that no tobacco was to be shipped without having first passed an inspection at one of the legally established inspection warehouses.

"The common knowledge that the past and present inspection laws had failed to prevent the importation of unmarketable tobacco, plus a long depression, had changed the attitude of many of the influential planters and merchants," wrote Virginia historian Melvin Herndon. "Nevertheless, the act did meet with opposition from some of the English customs officials and a few of the large planters."

Two inspectors were stationed at each warehouse. A third was summoned in case of a dispute between the two. These officials were bonded, and passing bad tobacco carried a heavy penalty. Inspectors were required to open the hogshead, extract two samples and carefully examine them. Trash and inferior tobacco were burned in the warehouse kiln. When the inspection

The interior of a tobacco barn. *Courtesy of the Library of Congress.*

was finished, the good tobacco was repacked in the hogshead. Then the planter's mark, weight and name of the inspection warehouse were stamped on the hogshead. Masters of all ships were required to take an oath that they would not load any casks that did not have an official stamp.

"This Tobo hath passed the Inspection of our new law," wrote a prominent planter in complaint to a London merchant. "Every hogshead was cased and viewed by which means the tobacco was very much tumbled and made something less sightly than it was before and it causes a great deal of extraordinary trouble."

After the new inspection law was passed, many planters were concerned that the inspections caused their hogsheads to be ransacked. Some expressed their concerns with words. Others resorted to violence. During the first year of the new law, two inspection houses were burned to the ground, one in Lancaster County and another in Northumberland. By 1732, though, Prince William County had become a hotbed of dissent.

Parliament. *Courtesy of the Library of Congress.*

Scots-Irish farmers in the western part of the county revolted against the law, mounting an armed rebellion that had drastic consequences.

The roots of the conflict dated back for generations, the vestige of a system of indentured servitude that grew increasingly criminal. During the colonial era, servants were imported from England and Northern Ireland. This allowed people with few resources to make the trip to the New World, although they had to enter into contracts under bond to work four or five years after their arrival. When that time expired, they took up lands of their own. But this class of newcomers lacked capital. So they sought the cheapest form of labor available: convicts. Under an act of Parliament in 1718, convicts could be "cast for transportation" to "the plantations." At first, the practice involved minor criminals. But by the 1720s, more and more violent criminals were being shipped over to work the plantations of Virginia.

"As for malefactors condemned to transportation," observed Robert Beverly in 1722, "tho' the greedy planters will always buy them, it is to be feared they will be very injurious to the county, which has already suffered many murders and robberies, the effect of that new law in England."

By 1732, the tension over the tobacco inspections was on the verge of violence—a phenomenon that was fueled in part by the criminal element that had now become a familiar part of the landscape. But the men who led the insurrection were not all backwoods criminals.

One of the leaders of the movement was Thomas Furr of Stafford County, who received a grant of more than one thousand acres at the head of Elk Run from Thomas Lord Fairfax. Also among the landed insurgents were James Bland and Henry Filkins, who were seated on the Occoquan in 1715. Fur and Filkins were among the band of fifty or so Scots-Irish insurgents who raided tobacco warehouses and burned harvested tobacco. They created such a furor that Governor Gooch ordered the militia to put down what later became known as the Prince William Rebellion.

It didn't take long for the long arm of the law to restore regular order, crushing the insurgency and dragging the guilty parties before a magistrate. The Colonial Council minutes for May 2, 1732, document the fallout:

> *James Bland, Thomas Furr, Thomas Furr the younger, together with Henry Filkins of said county to attend this board at the next court of Oyer and Terminer, held the second Tuesday in June and that all other persons concerned in the insurrection upon giving security for their future good behavior for one twelve month and one day, before the court of said county of Prince William be discharged from all further prosecution for their aforesaid offense.*

Tensions did not end when the governor crushed the insurgency; they just moved to the political realm. Politicians such as Thomas Osborne sought to build influence among western voters. But they found large planters opposing them at every turn, a political bloc led by Thomas Harrison. The rivalry between the Osborne faction of Prince William and the moneyed crowd led by Harrison was a frequent topic of conversation at the capital, where lawmakers regularly heard proposals to divide the county.

For folks in the west, these attempts were viewed as a way to divide and conquer. So they fought in the General Assembly just as bitterly as they had fought their rivals in the Prince William insurrection. Separate petitions to divide the county were considered in 1732, 1736, 1738, 1740 and 1742. All were rejected.

John Bull, baited by the dogs of excise. *Courtesy of the Library of Congress.*

EXCISE-OFFICE
At him! at him! Tally-ho, he, he
Kings' Yellow
New Excise Fetters for John Bull
EX-CISE

"It is interesting to note that our county has to some degree remained divided between residents of the east and west into the twentieth century," observed county historian George Brown, "although it would be neither fair nor correct to attribute it to these early difficulties."

6

Supervisors for Sale

Zoning Scandal Rocks Fairfax County

Corruption on the agenda for developers in the age of Camelot.

Customers who order a vanilla soy chai latte at the Bradlick Shopping Center Starbucks these days probably don't know that the land they are standing on brought down three elected leaders and a number of developers. And most of the residents at the Audubon Estates in the Mount Vernon part of Fairfax County probably don't realize that they're at the epicenter of a cash-for-zoning scandal that rocked Northern Virginia in the late 1960s—a scandal that eventually led to increased transparency of government officials.

All that came later, though.

At first, it was just a fistful of dollars and a heart full of greed. That's all it took for developers to lure members of the Fairfax County Board of Supervisors into casting favorable votes on a couple of controversial zoning matters. At issue were acres of old farmland that had skyrocketed in value during the go-go days of Camelot in the early 1960s, a time when citizens were seeing stars. Developers were seeing dollar signs. And life was not as innocent as the gauzy nostalgia of the era might suggest.

At the center of the scandal was John Poindexter Parrish, who represented the Mount Vernon magisterial district of the Fairfax County Board of Supervisors. A native of Washington, Parrish was a longtime resident of Fairfax County who graduated from the old Lee Jackson High School. During World War II, he served on navy destroyers in the

Zoning for Backlick Shopping Center was purchased with a bribe. *Courtesy of Liz Lynch.*

The *Alexandria Gazette* headquarters was burned down by Union occupiers during the Civil War. The side of the building is still charred today. *Courtesy of Liz Lynch.*

Atlantic and the Pacific. After the war, he received a law degree from George Washington University.

Although he lost his first election to the board of supervisors in 1955, he got himself appointed to a vacant seat in 1960 and quickly rose to prominence. By 1965, he was able to assume the position of chairman of the board on the promise that he would use a kitchen timer to keep a limit on long-winded speakers. By that time, though, he found himself enmeshed in a scandal that would eventually cost him his law license, his ability to participate in public life as an elected official and his part-time $7,500 gig on the county board.

The cash-for-zoning scandal happened at a time when city slickers were fleeing to the suburbs in a phenomenon known as "white flight." Neighborhoods across the sprawling suburbs of Fairfax County had cheap land and corrupt politicians willing to sell the necessary zoning. Elected members of the board of supervisors found themselves holding power that their predecessors could never have imagined as hundreds of new residents began demanding schools, housing, sewers and transportation. But the American dream was about to become the Fairfax nightmare.

Enter Til Hazel, a developer who arrived on the scene in 1960—right about the same time that Supervisor Parrish was learning his way to the men's room at the county government complex. It didn't take Hazel long to realize how the game was played. Cash greased the skids in Fairfax County, and developers who wanted to be successful learned the rules of the game. If they knew what was good for them, they contributed to their own success.

"We had a land-use system based upon politics and individual politicians votes," Hazel would later observe. "While the procedures were reasonably superficial, it was clear that influence with supervisors was critical. I did not accept that premise then or ever—there had to be rules for me to remain engaged. If you don't have rules, there is no preventing the potential for corruption."

Corruption was the order of the day in the early 1960s as the dark side of Camelot swept Fairfax County. By the time Parrish was making a name for himself as the newest supervisor in the Mount Vernon District, influence peddling had already become the coin of the realm in the smoke-filled rooms where zoning decisions were bought and sold like cheap cigars.

When President John Kennedy appointed his brother to lead the Justice Department, most of the headline writers focused on Bobby Kennedy's pursuit of the mob. Few realized that the attorney general would use anti-racketeering legislation to target politicians in the pocket of developers, a growing class of elected leaders in Fairfax County.

It all started so innocently. Developers wanted to build a medium-rise apartment complex in the Dranesville District just off Route 123. It couldn't have been a sweeter deal. First Lady Jackie Kennedy's stepfather owned a nearby estate known as Merrywood, a bucolic slice of Northern Virginia that overlooked the Potomac River at Chain Bridge Hill. Interior Secretary Stewart Udall lived nearby. The attorney general also lived in the neighborhood. So when a rezoning application for the apartment complex came before the board of supervisors, senior administration officials were watching closely.

Opponents of the rezoning argued that the land had significant historic value and that its scenic beauty would be undermined by a tacky apartment complex. Dransesville supervisor Armistead Claiborne Leigh was one of the first elected officials to oppose the rezoning effort, at least at first. But by the time the matter was on the docket, something had obviously persuaded Supervisor Leigh to change his mind. He voted in favor of the rezoning. This struck many observers as odd, including agents at the Internal Revenue Service. Agents with the local office began looking through tax returns and bank accounts.

John Poindexter Parrish. *Courtesy of Liz Lynch.*

"A can of worms was suddenly opened," said William Wrench, former director of the Fairfax County Economic and Industrial Development Committee.

Before long, a grand jury was impaneled. Bribery was investigated. Decisions were scrutinized. By the fall of 1966, prosecutors were ready to pull the trigger. On September 20, 1966, the grand jury handed down twenty-four zoning bribery conspiracy indictments. Caught in the web were fifteen county officials, developers and zoning attorneys. Eight of those were eventually convicted, including three members of the board of supervisors: John Poindexter Parrish, Armistead Claiborne Leigh and Robert Claude Cotton.

"They were taking bribes…for things like trailer parks, which you can't declare on your income tax," explained former delegate Jim Dillard, who represented Fairfax in the 1980s and '90s. "The other thing they would do is they would say, 'I'll vote against this new development in my district, but you all vote for it so it will pass. I can still claim I voted against it to please my constituents.'"

The problems started back in the summer of 1961, when a group of developers formed a company called Trailer Court Ventures and began making their generosity known. The rezoning was first approved on July 26, 1961, although it was later overturned by a court decision. Supervisors regranted the zoning the next summer, and the bribery payments were made from July 25, 1961, to September 15, 1961. Ultimately, the developers paid $5,500 to get the zoning they needed.

Another controversial rezoning involved land at the corner of Backlick and Braddock Roads, where developers wanted to build a shopping plaza. It was rezoned from single-family residential on a four-to-three vote even though the Planning Commission and county staff recommended against it. The developers cut Parrish a check—a payment that the chairman would later try to argue was part of an arrangement to purchase one thousand shares of stock in the shopping center. Jurors didn't buy that argument.

Parrish maintained his innocence throughout his trial, arguing that he received stock as part of an interest-free loan that he never attempted to repay. He was eventually found guilty of two counts of conspiracy for accepting $5,250 in stock in exchange for his vote to rezone land for the Bradlick Shopping Center in Annandale. The former chairman was sentenced to two years, and he served nine months in prison. He also lost his law license and his ability to participate in public affairs.

One of the high-profile figures arrested was Andrew Clarke, on Old Town Alexandria zoning attorney who served in the Virginia state senate from 1943 to 1951. He was charged with four counts of state bribery and two counts of federal bribery conspiracy. According to Audrey Moore, who would later become a supervisor, Clarke's bookkeeper "was very precise and made sure that everyone who took a bribe [was] paid after the rezoning so it would not look like a bribe."

But the evidence was there in black and white. Next to each of the illegal deals, Clarke's bookkeeper wrote "cost of zoning."

Clark was lucky. He had Til Hazel, who handled the former senator's defense. He argued that the conspiracy charge was unfounded because the action at the center of the charge happened before passage of the Anti-Racketeering Act.

"The statute, originally passed as a means to thwart organized crime, allowed the use of tax returns in criminal prosecutions," he explained. Clarke's "tax returns provided the basis for the prosecution, but these returns were filed in years prior to legislation."

Clarke suffered from Parkinson's disease, and he had already suffered several strokes by the time prosecutors had him in their sights. Hazel was able to persuade the judge to exclude Clark from trial based on his failing health.

"I brought in the chief pathologist from Georgetown Hospital to testify that Andy was, indeed, a very sick man and couldn't stand trial," said Hazel. "I believe his sickness clouded his judgment."

For many, the rise and fall of Andrew Clarke played out like some sort of Greek tragedy. He had once been one of the most powerful politicians in Northern Virginia, returning to private life only to become one of the most influential land-use attorneys in Fairfax County. Now, at the end of his career, he had become a sad and sick man who stood accused of selling power and influence for a few hundred dollars here and there. Clarke died in March 1968, never standing trial for the misdeeds prosecutors said he was guilty of perpetrating.

"After the IRS came in, it was apparent that the bribes were so little," explained Audrey Moore. "It is pitiful when you see major things happen because of so little money."

In a separate case, former supervisor Robert Claude Cotton was found guilty of accepting $3,000 for his vote to rezone land so a developer could build a trailer park—the genesis of Audubon Estates. During the trial, Cotton insisted that some of the money was a loan and some of the money was a campaign donation. In 1967, he was convicted of two counts of conspiracy to commit bribery and sentenced to two years in federal prison. Cotton was sentenced to two years but served time from August 1969 to January 1970.

Supervisor Claiborne Leigh also faced his own jury at the Alexandria federal courthouse. The former Dranesville supervisor was found guilty and sentenced to two years, although he ended up serving a fraction of the time at Allenwood Prison in Pennsylvania. The five developers caught up in the scandal were sentenced to a variety of terms, from eighteen months to two years.

Meanwhile, at the Massey building, Fairfax County government officials were trying to figure out a way to press forward with the public's business. But the legal jeopardy put the county in an awkward position. The business of government had to move forward, despite the ongoing legal battle between the federal prosecutors and the county's elected officials.

Zoning for Audubon Estates was purchased with a bribe. *Courtesy of Liz Lynch.*

"We had a meeting where we told those who had been indicted that we could not sit with them anymore," said Joseph Alexander, who was elected to represent the Lee District in 1964. "They weren't too happy about that, but we explained we [couldn't] do the people's business with them still in the room."

But conducting business as usual proved to be difficult if not impossible. Fairfax County had been tainted by scandal, and people began viewing everyone with suspicion.

"The scandal gutted the development process," said county planner Rosser Payne, who left the department as a result of the uncertainty created by the scandal. "It created a stigma on the whole process. We in the planning department didn't know what to do or how we could recover."

In the push and pull of development, critics will always emerge to oppose proposals. But the red-hot intensity of the 1960s zoning scandal gave opponents a powerful weapon. They could always argue that widespread corruption at the highest levels of county government were a force to be reckoned with, and they were right. The court case exposed the problems associated with government officials on the take, selling their votes in exchange for thirty pieces of silver.

In response to the growing concern about the county's integrity, the county facilitated the creation of an eight-member citizens committee to look into the zoning procedures and land-use system. The Zoning Procedures Study Committee included members of the business and development community, as well as civic groups and neighborhood associations. The idea was to make the process more "fair and efficient." So, naturally, one of the members was Til Hazel.

After a year of intense meetings and heated discussions, the group produced a report that suggested substantial changes on how the process worked. One of the biggest suggested changes would have undermined the ability of the board of supervisors to be the final authority on zoning changes. That kind of a change needed to be approved by the General Assembly, though, whose members were wary of making changes that were not supported by the supervisors.

"Unfortunately, the legislation and suggested changes were largely unsupported by the Board of Supervisors and proved to be merely an interesting discussion topic, despite substantial lip service to the contrary," Hazel wrote in 1976. "The supervisors...did not wish to divest themselves of the power of decision in land use matters at the zoning level."

Those who got caught up in the zoning scandal never made a comeback, but they did move on with their lives. After he was released from federal prison in 1969, Parrish went to work at Audubon Estates—the same Audubon Estates that was caught up in the zoning scandal when the developer bribed his way into rezoning eighty-three acres for a trailer park. Parrish spent his final years selling and renting trailers.

The legacy of the zoning scandal lives on today, even though the players are now off the scene and the events have largely been forgotten. Some of the reforms still linger, including the requirement that supervisors and developers disclose any interest they might have in a rezoning. But suspicions linger, even today. Many people wonder about the power and influence developers wield in the halls of Fairfax County government. These days, the bribery might not be overt. Wealth always finds a way to influence power, whether it's a donation to a favorite charity or a well-placed campaign contribution.

7

Fire and Brimstone

Occupiers Bully Old Town Alexandria

Union thugs invade St. Paul's, burn down newspaper.

During the darkest days of the Civil War, St. Paul's Episcopal Church in Old Town Alexandria was transformed into St. Paul's General Hospital for the sick and injured. Union soldiers and Confederate prisoners were laid out on the doors to the pews, which had been ripped from their hinges and laid over the tops of the rows as makeshift beds. A Yankee guard patrolled outside to keep order, according to an anecdote recorded by the late St. Paul's historian Ruth Lincoln Kaye.

"Hurrah for Jefferson Davis," a five-year-old girl who lived next to the occupied church yelled at the guard. "Hurrah for the South!"

Day after day, the patrolling Union guard would be harassed by the little girl. She would wave her Confederate flag and taunt the Yankee occupier with endless enthusiasm. Finally, the guard had had enough. He snapped.

"Hurrah for the devil!" he responded.

The Confederate girl was quick with a response.

"You cheer for your side, I'll cheer for mine!"

The conflict that led to the Civil War began as a political fight: the election of 1860. Everyone knows the Republican candidate that year—a former congressman from Illinois named Abraham Lincoln. Many are aware of one of the Democratic candidates: Stephen Douglas. Very few know that the Democratic Party was split in half and that Democrats in the South had their own candidate, Vice President John Breckinridge.

Exterior of St. Paul's Episcopal Church. *Courtesy of St. Paul's Episcopal Church.*

Almost nobody has heard of the candidate who was popular in Alexandria: John Bell.

Bell was a former Speaker of the House, former senator and former secretary of war when he launched his presidential campaign in 1860 as a candidate of the Constitutional Union Party. Although Bell was a Tennessee slave owner, he was one of the few Southern politicians to oppose the expansion of slavery in the 1850s.

Here in Alexandria, Unionists staged a series of evening meetings in support of Constitutional Union Party candidate Bell. Out on the campus of Episcopal High School, students organized political factions and raised flagpoles in honor of their presidential choice. Most of the students supported Bell, a third-party candidate who took a neutral stand on the issue of slavery. On election day, supporters paraded through Old Town with—what else?—bells of all sizes ringing into the evening.

John Bell won Alexandria. It was a landslide. But it wasn't enough for him to win the presidency. That went to a one-term congressman named Abraham Lincoln, a man with far less experience than Bell, Douglas or Breckinridge. Here in Alexandria, two newspapers followed the events closely. One was the *Virginia Sentinel*, which was pushing hard for secession.

The other was the older and more sedate *Alexandria Gazette*, which appealed to the Unionist sentiment. As the nation spiraled out of control, it was a good time for new business. By late November, reported *Gazette* editor Edgar Snowden, the rate of subscriptions for the last three months had never been higher in the paper's seventy-six-year history.

Gazette editor Edgar Snowden. *Courtesy of Louise Krafft.*

The election of Lincoln began a series of unfortunate events in the region. In Fairfax County, for example, a rowdy mob seized a known Lincoln supporter on the courthouse steps and escorted him out of town. Then they gave him a "blacking" with printer's ink, mounted him on his horse and pointed him home. The next month, the courthouse was once again seized by anti-Lincoln demonstrators. The crowd adopted several resolutions, castigating the election of Lincoln as an act of aggression against states' rights—and a direct attack on the institution of slavery.

Perhaps the most significant resolution adopted by the impromptu Fairfax assembly concluded that Virginia had a right to secede and resist the passage of coercive forces throughout the commonwealth. One man in the crowd raised his voice against the resolutions, saying they did not go far enough. That man was Alexandria's own James W. Jackson, proprietor of the Marshall House on King Street. He offered a couple resolutions of his own. As a result, the group ended up adopting a resolution declaring that Virginians who dared to hold federal offices in the Lincoln administration would be deemed "untrue" to the state. Yet another Jackson-inspired resolution declared that voters who cast ballots for black Republicans should "be requested to remove to the free states where they can find sympathizers."

So what should we make of this Fairfax mob legislature? Nothing like it happened in Alexandria, where newspapers urged more "peaceful measures for securing true independence and security" through an increase in home manufacturers. At best, those in attendance represented a radical fraction of the community. At worst, they represented a rowdy band of racists.

In any event, the assembly was an indication that the situation was quickly veering out of control. For more than a year, cities throughout Virginia had been endorsing new domestic enterprises in response to the heightened mood of secessionism sparked by John Brown's raid on Harper's Ferry. Merchants who failed to comply were risking it all. In Old Town, for example, King Street grocer James Stoutenburg raised suspicions that he was monopolizing Yankee trade. Irate Alexandrians even accused him of taking the *New York Tribune*! He was sternly cautioned to change his ways, if he knew what was good for him.

Lincoln's election had an immediate influence on the concept of homeland security in Alexandria, where three different volunteer units began drilling regularly: the Mount Vernon Guards, the Alexandria Rifleman and the Alexandria Artillery. By December, another group, known as the Old Dominion Rifles, formed and elected a captain.

Snow blanketed the ground in Alexandria on that cold December day when South Carolina seceded from the Union. The *Gazette* predicted that a bountiful ice crop that winter would free the city from a dependence on Northern supplies the following summer. By January, the Old Dominion Rifles had completed its organization, selected a gray uniform in Virginia-spun cloth and contracted with George Harper, a local tailor, to construct outfits for twenty-two dollars each. In Richmond, members of the General Assembly voted to hold a secession convention beginning on February 13—a sort of valentine for the commonwealth.

That meant one thing: politics. Every city, town and county had to elect delegates to the convention, which meant a fierce political fight over who would represent Alexandria. The contenders included George Brent, scion of the prominent Brent family of Virginia and the pro-Union candidate. Then there was David Funsten, the candidate of the secessionists. Brent said he could justify secession only if the federal government infringed on the rights of the state—a pretty vague standard. Funsten, on the other hand, pegged his vote on what was known as the Crittenden Compromise—a congressional debate that was very closely followed in its day and almost totally lost today. In essence, it called for the permanent reinstatement of the former Missouri Compromise line at latitude 36°30', prohibiting slavery in the Northern states while giving Southerners an option. The House passed the compromise, but it stalled in the Senate—which Funsten said meant Virginia should secede.

Tempers flared at a meeting of workingmen and mechanics the night of January 28 at Liberty Hall. The *Gazette* described the audience as the largest indoor assembly in the city's history. Most of the men in attendance were there to support the Union, which led to fervent shouts of "We ain't going to secede!" and "Damn the palmetto flag!"

A mass of Alexandria residents gathered at the Catalpa Parade Grounds at the northwest corner of Pendleton and North Washington Streets—today the home of a Bank of America—to fire off the town mascot. This was a small cannon, probably about thirty inches long, known as the Little Coon Killer because, as they said at the time, it was barely big enough to kill a raccoon and probably not even that.

By the way, the cannon is now in the possession of the Masons and stored at the Masonic temple.

Alexandria, like much of the country, was divided. Many St. Paul's families left town rather than take the oath of allegiance. Among those who left was Rector George Norton, namesake of the fellowship hall at St. Paul's. Another man who left town was the rector emeritus James Johnston—the man for whom the Johnston Room at the church is named. Norton went to Lexington, where he served at St. Peter's Episcopal Church, now known as Grace Episcopal Church. Johnston went to Charlottesville and later Richmond, although he apparently returned to Alexandria occasionally to officiate at baptisms and funerals.

After Union soldiers invaded Alexandria and seized control in May 1861, many of Alexandria's churches were closed, with the exception of Christ Church, which was kept open for army chaplains. Congregants who were loyal to the Union—and there were some—continued attending services there. But members of Christ Church who were loyal to the Southern cause began attending services at St. Paul's.

The problem was that St. Paul's was closed.

Church leaders hopped around town to various locations—Sarepta Hall, Liberty Hall, Phoenix Hall, American Hall and, ultimately, the Odd Fellows Hall. By November 1861, leaders at St. Paul's had decided to throw caution to the wind and conduct services on church property. So they met in the Lecture Hall, a building located where Wilmer Hall stands today. Services were held on Wednesday nights and Sunday nights. That went off without a hitch, so services were moved back into the sanctuary.

To be clear, church leaders were playing with fire. They knew the Union occupiers did not want them to meet in the sanctuary. They knew the Union soldiers were heavily armed. And they knew a bunch of

Confederate supporters gathered for services would invite suspicion. But they did it anyway.

So one unseasonably warm day in January 1862, St. Paul's Episcopal Church reopened for service. The sermon that day focused on Psalm 9:9: "The Lord, also, will be a refuge for the oppressed, a refuge in times of trouble."

The service was slightly altered, though. The people conspicuously omitted a prayer for the president of the United States of America. It's worth noting that the leaders of St. Paul's could have included a prayer for President Davis. But they didn't do that, either. They simply left that part out of the service altogether, a choice that caused a stir in town. When word got to Alexandria's military governor, General Montgomery, he summoned two St. Paul's leaders to his office for an explanation. Eventually, the general concluded that the issue did not warrant official notice as long as the church was not engaging in "seditious language to prove disaffection to the government."

With that, church leaders thought they had been given the go-ahead. But trouble was brewing. Within weeks, St. Paul's would experience the most dramatic service ever in the church's history. The date—Sunday, February 9, 1862—will live in infamy.

It started pleasantly enough. Congregants—mostly women and children—gathered here for services. The Reverend Kensey Johns Stewart was conducting services that day. But there was a snake in the garden. One of the pews near the chancel was occupied by the military, and soldiers were scattered throughout the church. Everyone was waiting for the prayers of the people. That part of the litany came and went without an appearance by President Lincoln, so a detective agent of the United States government ordered Stewart to pray at his dictation. Stewart ignored the order, so Captain Elon Farnsworth leapt to his feet and began reciting a prayer for the president.

Then, the quiet Episcopal service erupted into complete pandemonium.

The soldiers marched up to the chancel, where Stewart was still kneeling, continuing with the litany. When one of them laid his hand on Stewart's shoulder, warden James Green seized the officer and threw him out of the chancel. The soldier drew his revolver and pointed it at Green.

The altar was moments away from bloodshed. Fortunately, though, cooler heads prevailed. Farnsworth grabbed Stewart and announced that he was being arrested for omitting the prayer for the president of the United States on grounds that he was "a rebel and a traitor."

As Union soldiers invaded St. Paul's during a service, a lady in the choir gallery hurled a prayer book at the head of a Yankee. *Courtesy of St. Paul's Episcopal Church.*

"And I summon you," responded Stewart, "to answer at the judgment seat of the King of Kings and Lord of Lords for interfering, by force of arms, with his ambassador, while in the act of presenting the petitions of His people at His altar."

The soldiers forced the prayer book out of his hands, but Stewart continued the litany from memory as armed soldiers swarmed the sanctuary, sabers and revolvers in hand. Stewart tried to stand his ground, but Farnsworth dragged him by force from the altar down the center aisle.

As they passed under the west gallery, a lady of the choir hurled a prayer book at the head of the Yankee and missed. What might have happened if she had hit the Union solider?

In her book about the history of St. Paul's, Ruth Lincoln Kaye asked a different question: "Was she a soprano or an alto?"

Nobody will ever know the answer to that question. But we do know that Stewart was still wearing his surplice as he was dragged through the streets to Farnsworth's quarters. As he passed over the bricks, one woman—prayer

Gazette House. *Courtesy of Liz Lynch.*

book in hand—loudly berated the officers. Another woman put a roll of banknotes into Stewart's hands, explaining that he would probably need it. Then, the bewildered congregation dispersed.

General Montgomery was attending services at Christ Church as all of this was happening on the other side of Old Town. When word reached him about what had happened, he immediately telegraphed Washington for orders. Eventually, he was instructed to release Stewart.

The *Alexandria Gazette* detailed these events the next day at great length, creating an incendiary situation. An angry mob of Union thugs appeared outside the *Gazette* building around the corner on Prince Street and set fire to the building. Even today, the burn marks from that fire can be seen on the east wall of that building on Prince Street—a tangible reminder that the scars of the Civil War are still with us today.

St. Paul's was converted into a hospital facility, as were most of the city's larger buildings. Members of St. Paul's resumed services at the lecture hall on the corner along with members of Christ Church and Grace Episcopal Church. They continued to conduct services there for two years, until the Union army confiscated the building for its ever-growing series of hospitals to warehouse the dead and dying. Bodies were taken out behind the sanctuary, where the Union army constructed a morgue that still stands today. The current rector of St. Paul's, Oran Warder, says his boys had a grand time playing in the morgue as children.

From the summer of 1862 to the spring of 1865, the sanctuary was St. Paul's General Hospital for Union soldiers and Confederate prisoners. All the pews were used as beds. The organ in the west gallery became a medicine chest. The Lecture Hall became the surgeon's quarters. A mess house was constructed between the church and the Lecture Hall where the playground is now located.

The hospital had about 120 beds. The first batch of sick patients arrived on June 28, 1862. By the end of the year, more than six hundred patients had been admitted. An average list included fifty-three sick, three wounded and thirty wounded in action. During the occupation, one Union soldier left his signature for all of eternity on the Nelly Custis Bible, a gift of Major Laurence Lewis and Nelly Custis Lewis in 1832. The act of vandalism, still evident on the back page of the book, reads, "February 12, 1862. George LeSchell. O Sergeant of Company J."

That's not the only scar that was left by the war. The Confederate statue at Prince and South Washington lists twelve young men from St. Paul's who died in the Lost Cause. The war ended in 1865, when Lee surrendered to Grant at the home of Wilmer McLean, the son of one of the original founders of St. Paul's. After the war, he returned to Alexandria, where he and his wife are buried at the Old St. Paul's Cemetery with a grave inscribed to the mysterious Female Stranger. Three weeks after the surrender, services resumed at St. Paul's—at the Lecture Hall.

The first service included a prayer for the president of the United States of America.

8

Monte Carlo No More

Crime and Corruption in Rosslyn and Del Ray

Shotgun wielding prosecutor transforms Northern Virginia.

The posse of six men met on a Sunday in May 1904 and boarded the Alexandria and Mount Vernon Railroad southbound across the Long Bridge. Once the streetcar was in motion, Alexandria County commonwealth's attorney Crandal Mackey dumped several sacks in the aisle full of axes, guns and sledgehammers. For the crusading prosecutor who hoped to transform Rosslyn and Del Ray, these were the weapons of progress. As arranged, the conductor made a special stop.

The raid was on, and Crandal Mackey was about to transform Northern Virginia.

Mackey was an iconoclast, a reformer and an outcast. He won election as the commonwealth's attorney for Alexandria County—most of which is now known as Arlington County—in 1903 with a two-vote margin of victory. That's a difficult mandate for any elected official, especially one who wanted to overturn the machine that ran Virginia at the dawn of the twentieth century. Instead of second-guessing himself, though, Mackey grabbed his shotgun and conducted a series of raids with a posse of men carrying axes and shovels.

It wasn't an easy fight. Gambling had deep roots in Virginia and the psychology of Alexandria. Part of the money to finance the colony of Virginia came from a game of chance, a lottery approved by King James I in 1612. George Washington himself bought and sold lottery tickets,

Crandal Mackey. *Courtesy of the Virginia Room, Arlington Library.*

including snatching up the first ticket for the first federal lottery in 1793. The public wharves on the waterfront in Alexandria were built using revenue from lottery tickets.

Not only did Crandal Mackey have to work against that deep-seated human impulse to gamble, but he also had to take on some of the highest and lowest men of his era. He faced down two-bit gamblers. He closed saloons. He got into fistfights with railroad lawyers. And he fought the machine. In the end, his own party turned against him. It wasn't quite a rejection of what he had accomplished, although even today we can hear echoes that the reform movement was just some kind of misguided adventure.

"After the war, do-gooders forced the reluctant police to raid and close down the public gambling houses," observed Alexandria historian Frederick Tilp.

Clearly, Tilp had Mackey in mind when he wrote those words. Others view the Mackey legacy in more flattering terms.

"Arlingtonians owe a great debt of gratitude to Crandal Mackey and his group of civic crusaders," concluded Arlington historian Eleanor Lee Templeman.

In the end, Mackey's record is somewhat mixed. He shut down the violent dens in Rosslyn. He wiped a shantytown known as Jackson City near the Long Bridge off the map forever. But he also let the corrupt politicians walk, as long as they closed their gambling operations and went about their business as if nothing had happened. Nothing to see here, folks. Perhaps that's why enemies in his own party ended up taking him out in the end.

Then, in 1915, Crandal Mackey mysterioulsy abandoned his campaign for reelection. Nobody really knows why. Was it because he

Prosecutor Crandal Mackey conducted raids with his prized shotgun, now on display at the Arlington County Sheriff's office. *Courtesy of Brandy Crist-Travers.*

A group of barrooms in Rosslyn. *Courtesy of the Virginia Room, Arlington Library.*

was threatened? Newspapers from the era were full of stories about the prosecutor and his family receiving regular threats of violence. Did they shut him down? Was commonwealth's attorney Crandal Mackey silenced? Unfortunately, no one is alive today who can answer that question. The heavy hand of time has obscured the true crime story about this crusading prosecutor and the shotgun he wielded with a sense of frontier justice.

Again and again, lawyers representing some of the most powerful forces in Virginia politics went after the commonwealth's attorney from Alexandria County. They tried to delay. They tried to obfuscate. They tried to bribe. They tried violence and politics, sometimes at the same time.

"Elections in those days resulted in opponents labeling each other with rather pointed nicknames and sometimes using gunfire," wrote Templeman. "In one election the defeated candidate for sheriff announced that he was going out to kill Mackey, whom he felt had worked against him. With calm courage, Mackey ignored the threat."

Crandal Mackey believed in this sort of shotgun justice. Back-alley gamblers were as much at risk as elected officials on the take. Just as the tortoise slowly worked toward his goals in Aesop's fable, here was a man who was willing to wait for the fickle finger of fate.

Exiting the streetcar on the day of his infamous raid, Mackey led his armed posse to a high board fence around their first target, a place the *Evening Star* described as a "building in which all kinds of games were in the habit of being conducted." Fortunately for the armed posse, unsuspecting gamblers left the gate open. According to the *Star*'s eyewitness account of the raid, the gamblers all "suddenly recalled that they had other engagements."

The mad dash for the exits must have been chaotic.

"It did not bother them whether they left through the open doors or the closed windows," the *Star* reported.

But the raiders were disappointed. A thorough search of the place failed to uncover any bookmaking. Instead, they ended up busting a poker game. So the posse headed for Heath's place, the infamous gambling establishment on the banks of the Potomac River opposite Georgetown University. There they were confronted by Eddie Heath, proprietor of the infamous hillside gambling parlor.

Heath stood at the door with his shotgun. Mackey rushed up and disarmed him.

When they entered the downstairs, the raiding party discovered poker tables and a bar. Upstairs, they found the faro bank, the crap table, the hazard board and the keno tables. The deputized men in the raiding party then hacked up the bars, drained bottles of "ardent spirits," destroyed the slot machines, wrecked a policy wheel and, of course, gathered evidence. In the chaos, someone toppled a music box that began to play "There'll Be a Hot Time in the Old Town Tonight."

Unfortunately for Mackey, the raiding party found only one or two employees and two or three patrons. Only a couple of tables were in operation. Newspapers speculated that Sheriff Palmer might have tipped Heath off to the raid.

"The statement that Heath had been tipped off by a member of my staff is absolutely false," Palmer responded to a reporter for the *Washington Post*. "First for the reason that no one, not even the deputies in question knew of the contemplated raid, and second…that if it had been known that a raid was to be made, the games would not have been in progress."

Whether that was the case, much of Heath's gaming paraphernalia was not around when the raid went down. Apparently, he stashed his devices in Washington—far from the long arm of the law—waiting for a day when it would be safe on the other side of the Potomac River once again. A few token items were confiscated, and Heath was arrested along with two of his employees.

"I am not advised as to whether or not any gambling paraphernalia had been removed to Washington," said Sheriff Palmer. "I would say, however, that it would have been advisable to do so owing to the proximity of the premises to the residence of the commonwealth's attorney."

Hell's Bottom. *Courtesy of the Virginia Room, Arlington Library.*

From Heath's, the posse moved south to Jackson City, the infamous hellhole on the Virginia side of the Long Bridge. When they arrived, one of the deputies caused some uneasiness when he discharged his revolver to frighten a fleeing black man.

"Some of those in the party were anxious to apply the torch," the *Star* reported, "but Mackey would not countenance such conduct."

Instead, the commonwealth's attorney oversaw a path of destruction.

"They cut down the paintings, hacked the walls, broke the chairs and all the beautiful furniture, the tables, everything," recalled Frank Ball. "They just cut it into pieces."

In the end, the posse "made a demonstration which is intended to give the lawbreakers an idea of what they may expect if they persist," the *Star* reported. The deputies then set their sights on an infamous saloon operated by Jimmy Lafontaine at the south end of the Long Bridge. Lafontaine was arrested along with two associates, Charles Sanderson and Pat Ready.

"It is contended by Lafontaine and his two associates that Ready was cleaning up the bar at the time of the raid, and there was no gaming going on," the *Washington Times* reported.

The raids made Mackey an instant celebrity. His face was plastered across newspapers, and his name became synonymous with cleaning up crime and corruption. He was an instant legend or villain, depending on your point of view. For the reform set, he was a white knight in shining armor. For the corrupt politicians and saloon managers, he was the devil incarnate.

"I will close them," he bragged to the *Washington Post*, "even if I have to ask the governor to station a squad of soldiers in every gambling resort in the county."

Dealing with the St. Asaph Racetrack was more difficult.

The St. Asaph Racetrack offered more than a cheap bottle of booze or an easy lady of the night. It had glamour and gambling. Wealth and power. Graft and greed. Political corruption and telegraph wires. St. Asaph was no saint.

The idea that eventually became the St. Asaph Racetrack had its origins back in 1888, when the Gentleman's Driving Club was chartered. By 1893, leaders in Virginia had become alarmed about gambling in the commonwealth. So the General Assembly began talking about following suit. Alexandria County gamblers traveled to Richmond to lobby legislators in a bid to carve out an exemption that could give them a competitive advantage. It worked. Corrupt legislators ended up adding a provision creating an exemption for driving clubs, agricultural organizations or grange associations.

The St. Asaph Racetrack. *Courtesy of the Virginia Room, Arlington Library.*

Trustees of the Alexandria Driving Club included some of the most prominent men in town: William Daingerfield, Reverdy Daingerfield, George Uhler, Park Agnew and Virginia senator George Mushback. John Marriott Hill, who managed the city's opera house and a printing establishment, was in charge of the betting. Livery stable owner James Patterson became the chief promoter. Investors dumped $100,000 into making the facility a first-class endeavor.

For visitors, the park offered a panorama of sorts. On the right, visitors could see the hills of Virginia. On the left, in the distance, the Maryland shore was visible. And there, smack dab in the center, was the Potomac River. Because of the arrangement of the stables and grandstand, which faced south, the horses were never out of sight. Horses and guests alike had access to the best and purest water around. President Emanuel Downham and Secretary H.D. McIntyre made it clear that this organization was going to be legitimate by hiring "a strong force" of Pinkerton detectives to work the betting lawn and grandstand.

"No improper character will be permitted within the enclosure," the *Washington Post* reported, "the dominant idea of the promoters of this enterprise being that the ladies and gentlemen can attend the races without the slightest fear of being brought in contact with obnoxious or disreputable characters."

The reason for the warning was clear: gambling would play a central role at the racetrack. That meant a special effort by promoters to make sure visitors knew that crookedness was not to be tolerated, although there was a sense in later years that the sanctimonious message was delivered with a wink and a nod. Promoters told newspapermen that nothing in Virginia law prevented racing and "pool selling," essentially places where betting polls were operated. The recently enacted Mushback law—as it was known because of its chief sponsor, Virginia senator George Mushback—was aimed at the riffraff who congregated at Jackson City. Behind the scenes, though, Mushback was a corrupt politician who used his power and influence in Richmond to benefit his own interest in the racetrack.

Before Mackey could even attempt a raid on the racetrack, he wanted to lay the groundwork. That meant exposing the insiders' game that was being played at St. Asaph.

"The gambling ring is a bigger thing than many people believe," Mackey told the *Washington Post*. "The St. Asaph ring has been a power so potent in Virginia and particularly in Alexandria County that for years every one of the 22 delegates from the county in a gubernatorial convention has voted for their candidate."

Mackey went on to explain that some backers of the betting poolroom didn't go near the place for weeks or months at a time, but he knew almost all of them anyway.

"I believe I can lay my hands on people who can and will give the kind of testimony I want at the proper time," Mackey boasted.

Mackey knew that conducting a raid on St. Asaph would require more foresight than simply showing up with an axe-wielding posse.

To gain an exclusive indictment against the St. Asaph Racetrack, Mackey released the grand jury to place its own bets and gather firsthand evidence. The day after the raid on Rosslyn and Jackson City, Mackey issued nineteen warrants for men believed to be responsible for bookmaking and gaming at the St. Asaph Racetrack. Charges were filed against some of the leading members of the Hill-Jones syndicate that ran the infamous poolrooms.

"It is understood that the Hills will make no resistance but will agree to arrest," the *Washington Times* reported. "It is also rumored that they have employed some of the best legal talent in Washington, Baltimore and Richmond, Va., to represent them at the trials."

The Alexandria County courthouse. *Courtesy of the Virginia Room, Arlington Library.*

When all the smoke cleared, only six men were arrested—a disappointingly small outcome for such a well-orchestrated dragnet effort. Some speculated that Sheriff Palmer might have been working against the effort, tipping off the gambling interests and undercutting the success of the raids. All six men were taken before a justice of the peace and released on bail to appear in court the following Wednesday.

After the raids, tension began to build between Mackey and Palmer. According to news accounts, the prosecutor was angry with the sheriff for serving the warrants on the poolroom operators at St. Asaph without arresting any of the men he found there.

"The lawyer remarks that either the sheriff does not know his duty, or else he does not care to perform it," the *Washington Times* reported.

From that point on, Mackey announced, he would be serving warrants himself. The arrangement was not unprecedented, and newspapers compared the situation in Alexandria County to William Travers Jerome of New York, a prosecutor who also served his own warrants. Palmer, meanwhile, was compared to the infamously crooked New York City police chief William Stephen Devery.

"Certainly this looks as if Alexandria County were assuming a real metropolitan aspect, while Sheriff Palmer is certainly getting in line to compare notes with Big Chief Bill Devery when they meet on the other side of the great divide," the *Washington Times* noted.

By the middle of May, the legal fight had begun to take shape. Justice of the Peace Hagan issued warrants against eighteen men. They were charged with violating the anti-gambling laws of Virginia. The men immediately put together a stellar legal team, including the same lawyers who had fought Mackey when he was first elected. The legal trio went on the offensive. Appearing in Alexandria County court, the lawyers said Justice Hagan should be banned from the case because he had not qualified by taking the oath of office and giving bond. They also attacked irregularities in the warrants and charged that the campaign against their clients was unconstitutional.

"The gamblers have money and will spend it," the *Washington Times* reported. "Mackey has brains and nerve and, so far, he has proven equal to the occasion."

Strangely, the *Alexandria Gazette* engaged in selective reporting of the raid on the racetrack. The May 20, 1904 issue carried a one-paragraph notice under the headline "Wires Cut Out." Amazingly, the paragraph made no mention of the newly elected commonwealth's attorney or his crusade against gambling and corruption. It was a curious way to report events, especially considering all the ink thrown at Crandal Mackey by the *Times*, the *Star* and the *Post*.

"Wires and telegraph instruments of the Western Union company were removed from the St. Asaph poolroom yesterday," the *Gazette* noted. "The poolroom employees stated that they would have satisfactory arrangements for handling returns completed in a few days, but what their plans are they declined to disclose."

Yet the *Gazette* reported that the poolroom would have agents of its own at all the tracks who would be filing race results at telegraph stations nearest their respective tracks. Those returns would be received at the nearest office to St. Asaph. Because it was a common carrier, the *Gazette* reported, it would have to handle this business.

County officials picked up envelopes full of cash at the old Klondike place. *Courtesy of the Virginia Room, Arlington Library.*

"Receiving returns in this manner will necessitate a string of messenger boys from the telegraph office to the poolroom, and the results cannot be made known so quickly as heretofore," the *Gazette* explained. "It is not known how soon these arrangement can be perfected."

It was clear that powerful and unseen forces were at work. In the courtroom, the legal team for the racetrack sought to gain a writ of prohibition—essentially shutting down the prosecution. And it was successful. On May 12, Judge Nicol granted the writ of prohibition. That was a strategy used over and over again against Mackey, with mixed results. For now, at least, gaining the writ of prohibition succeeded in kicking the can down the road and postponing the case until at least June. Despite Nicol's ruling, Mackey told the *Washington Post* that the judge was one of the "cleanest men and foremost jurists of Virginia, who has no superior at the bar."

By the end of May, gambling was lively again in Northern Virginia. Rosslyn may have been quieted, and the Western Union lines at St. Asaph may have gone cold, but the Long Bridge Monte Carlo wasn't dead yet. The *Washington Times* reported that Jackson City was already going "at full blast." Sweat boards, policy and crap games were being

This cartoon was published on the front page of the *Washington Times* on January 13, 1905. *Courtesy of the Virginia Room, Arlington Library.*

conducted by some of the same men who had been raided only a few days before. Apparently, they feared nothing from the long arm of the law.

Crandal Mackey did not stop with the raids. He fought the long and difficult fight in the courtroom, helping to overturn the political machine that ran the state in those days. By the time he retired from office in 1915, he had become a legend. Arlington County once had a park named in his honor, although now it has been reduced to rubble to facilitate construction of a new development in Rosslyn. Hopefully, it will include some kind of reminder of the hidden history of Alexandria County.

9

The Code Duello

Henry Clay Versus John Randolph in Arlington

Mania of dueling comes to Alexandria, D.C.

Parson Weems called it "mania" that was gripping the young nation. Tucked away in a dusty archive at the Library of Congress is an obscure manuscript from 1820 in which Weems castigates "the Code," also known as "the Code Duello." He described it as "a fit of madness" engaged in by men who led "foolish and disorderly [lives], terminating as [they] everlastingly [do], in misery."

Oftentimes, an intense foreplay preceded the duel—one that frequently spilled out on the pages of the newspaper. And the *Alexandria Gazette* was no exception, printing accusations and counter-accusations in the parry and riposte of those whom Weems described as "the bloody minded and distempered beasts who are always picking quarrels and writing challenges." The telltale signs were "the scornful nose, the supercilious brow and the bold impudent loquacity."

"Call it chagrin, call it hate, malice, revenge, or by whatever name you please, it is misery still, that puts men up to dueling," Weems wrote. "If they can't muster patience to wait long enough to kill themselves with whiskey and tobacco, they will give way to their brutish passions and provoke some other madman to blow out their brains."

Virginia's most famous duel took place in 1826 between two heavyweights in American politics: Secretary of State Henry Clay and United States senator John Randolph of Roanoke. The dispute between the two started as

Henry Clay. *Courtesy of the Library of Congress.*

John Randolph. *Courtesy of the Library of Congress.*

an honest disagreement over foreign policy, sparked when the Speaker of the House refused to entertain Virginia's resolution against a declaration of war. Eventually, the secretary of state challenged the Virginia senator to a duel. Mutual friends of both parties tried to intervene and smooth things over, but to no avail.

Saturday, April 8, 1826, was chosen as the date. Unlike other duels involving prominent Alexandrians of the era, this duel actually took place in Alexandria, D.C.—modern-day Arlington County—at the request of Randolph. He wanted the duel to take place in Virginia because if he was killed, he said, he wanted to fall on the soil "endeared to him by every tie of devoted loyalty and affection." So the participants agreed on a spot in a dense forest on the Virginia side of the Potomac just above the Little Falls Bridge—today the location of the Chain Bridge.

Pistols were chosen as the weapon on choice. Half past 4:00 p.m. was chosen as the time. The distance would be ten paces, and each party would be attended by two seconds and a surgeon. No practice rounds would be allowed. These gentlemen were playing for keeps. Clay's seconds were Colonel Thomas Jessup and Senator Josiah Johnston of Louisiana. Randolph's seconds were Colonel Edward Tattnal of Georgia and General James Hamilton of South Carolina.

The night before the duel, Randolph paid a visit to General Hamilton to chat about the firefight. The senator seemed incredibly relaxed for a man who would be facing the business end of a pistol the next morning at forty paces.

"Hamilton, I have determined to receive, without returning, Clay's fire; nothing shall induce me to harm a hair of his head," Randolph told Hamilton. "I will not make his wife a widow, or his children orphans. Their tears would be shed over his grave, but when the sod of Virginia rests on my bosom, there is not in the wide world one individual to pay this tribute upon mine."

Randolph's friends thought this plan was insane and tried to talk him out of it. But the senator was stubborn, and he had already charted his course for the duel. Their attempts were in vain.

"If I see the devil in Clay's eye," Randolph said, "I may change my mind."

On the day of the duel, participants arrived at the appointed time and place—near the modern-day intersection of Military Road and Glebe Road. The sun was setting, and Randolph apparently found no devil in Clay's eye. Yet he was confronting a man who possessed a fearless and vigilant purpose of mind. Here were two giants of American politics, facing each other on the field of battle. The ground was marked off for the duel, and the principals saluted each other courteously. Each took his respective place on an east and west line. Clay was in front of a small stump, while Randolph was near a low, gravelly embankment. Colonel Tattnal handed Randolph his pistol and sprung the hair-trigger.

"Tattnal, although I am one of the best shots in Virginia, with either a pistol or a gun, yet I never fire with a hair-trigger," Randolph said. "Besides, I have a thick buckskin glove on which will destroy the delicacy of my touch, and the trigger may fly before I know where I am."

But the colonel insisted. When the secretary and the senator took their positions, Randolph's pistol went off before the word was given. Fortunately, the muzzle was down. But Colonel Jessup said that he would leave the field if that happened again, even though Clay said it was clearly an accident. Randolph was handed another pistol. Then both principals exchanged shots. Randolph's bullet struck a stump behind Clay. And Clay's shot kicked up a bit of earth and gravel behind Randolph. Each side reloaded, and Clay fired a shot that knocked up gravel behind Randolph. Then Randolph raised his pistol and fired into the air.

"I do not fire at you, Mister Clay," the senator said.

With that, the senator approached the secretary of state across the dueling field and extended his hand. The secretary responded enthusiastically, and the two men shook hands. Even though Randolph's coat had been pierced by one of Clay's shots, the feud had obviously come to an end.

"You owe me a coat, Mister Clay," Randolph said.

"I am glad the debt is no greater," Clay responded.

10

Ark of the Commonwealth

Floating Brothels Service Old Town

Between the devil and the deep blue sea on the Potomac River.

Batten down the hatches. Beat to quarters. A wicked tale is brewing along the waterfront in Alexandria.

It's a story about the world's oldest profession setting up shop along the deepwater port in Old Town, hundreds of floating brothels swiftly moving up and down the Potomac Yard to avoid the long arm of the law. The golden age of fast women and floating streetwalkers was the twentieth century, a time when the shores along the District of Columbia waterfront became too crowded to handle the crush of floating brothels there. When the D.C. Harbor Police built barricades, the fleet of strumpets headed south.

"Customers from foreign vessels anchored near Alexandria's wharves made this waterfront the most profitable location for ark-girls," wrote Admiral Frederick Tilp, official historian of the Old Town waterfront. "Several packet steamship companies running the downtown route and ending in Baltimore or Norfolk worked out a *deal* with the well-organized *houses* in Alexandria to be furnished two girls each week, one for all-night service and another for the *quickie* jobs."

Illicit maritime commerce has a long and storied history in the Chesapeake Bay, an empire built on oysters and crabs. During colonial days, the natives called Captain Henry Fleet a "loose liver." He chased the sailor's bait up and down the beautiful shores of the Potomac, setting the scene for centuries of dingy harlots. Even before the Civil War, the waterfront had a reputation for being a hotbed of hot beds. By dawn of the twentieth century, the Washington Harbor was like a Grand Central terminal for the midnight packet trade. Tilp identifies nine of the most notorious floating brothels:

CIVILIAN TRADE

The Foggy Bottom
arrival: Washington City Canal at Constitution Avenue
departure: Rock Creek Mole

The Hamburgh
arrival: Washington City Canal at Constitution Avenue
departure: Capitol

The Jackson City
arrival: Washington and Old Dominion terminal
departure: Jackson City

The Murder Bay
arrival: Washington City Canal at Constitution Avenue
departure: Capitol

MILITARY FLEET

The Arsenal Grounds
arrival: Fort McNair
departure: Fort McNair

The Buzzard Point
arrival: Fort McNair
departure: Navy Yard

The Carrolsburg
arrival: Fort McNair
departure: Navy Yard

The Pipetown
arrival: Navy Yard
departure: Benning Bridge

The Uniontown
arrival: Anacostia
departure: Anacostia

As the capital city grew increasingly crowded and industrialized, the District locations became cesspools of wastewater. The Washington City Canal and the Benning Bridge were essentially open sewers, increasingly fetid and unbearable. A catastrophic series of floods reduced Rosslyn and Georgetown to wastelands. So the vice captains of industry turned their attention south, assuming that authorities in Virginia and Maryland were too busy chasing oyster pirates to care about a bunch of bawdy houseboats.

Ark cities washed in and washed out with the daily tide. Military men accounted for about half the trade, especially the artillerymen overseeing the big guns at Fort Washington. They boarded vessels headed to points near and far, and the journey was always more important than the destination. Time seemed to stand still near the tobacco warehouse at Broad Creek or just past Hatton Point on Swan Creek. Patrons from Fort Humphreys headed for Gunston Cove, and the men from Fort Hunt ducked into Piscaway Creek.

The most popular venue was Bull Town Cove, a notorious spot directly across from Mount Vernon. For outlaws seeking to outsmart the law, the geography was alluring. It also happened to be the boundary between Prince George's County and Charles County, a perfect way to make lawbreaking somebody else's problem.

"Friendly farmers living on surrounding hills proved to be an effective bulwark as Bull Town Cove was never raided," explained Admiral Tilp. "Law enforcement was negligible and the location of the houseboats at the edge of the deep water channel was a convenient place for watermen to stop and buy a little *fun* at a lower price than in the nation's capital."

Another infamous ark city formed at Oxon Creek, just past Fox Ferry Pont. It became a favorite for Firth Sterling Plant steelworkers and enlisted men from the U.S. Marine barracks seeking fringe benefits. From Rosslyn to Jones Point, the floating brothels along the Virginia shore were almost always one-woman affairs. Each madam was essentially the captain of her own ship, which was docked wherever demand was greatest at the time. A lower-class whorehouse had a red roof and red shutters. Quality anchorages

A floating brothel. *Courtesy of Frederick Tilp's* This Was Potomac River.

were painted white and had blue shutters with matching blue wooden finial along the roof ridge.

"A few of the better floating houses were moored near gambling barges off Jones Point or off Alexandria's ferry dock or at Jackson City," concluded Tilp. "There were several smaller ark colonies in the womanizing business near Aqueduct Bridge for the poor to fair Georgetown trade."

The scene was too much for the newshounds at the *Alexandria Gazette* to ignore. In 1905, the newspaper sent an enterprising reporter to cover the story:

> *The two-story houseboat* Dream, *anchored off Jones Point was lashed severely yesterday by a terrible northwest storm. She rode out the gale-like disturbance as safely as the* Ark *of the Bible. The boat, popular with many Alexandrians, dragged anchor, coming to a halt off Fort Foote, a distance of a mile or so to the southeast. The* Dream, *driven by strong blasts, was saved only through efforts of sympathetic fishermen in Great Hunting Creek.*
>
> *The scenes of revelry aboard were not checked by the wild outside elements, as small boats contained during the day and night, carrying patrons to and fro. It is said that the* Dream*'s owner is an enterprising female who has long been well-known in Alexandria.*
>
> *She is presently having another piece of architecture constructed at a prominent city shipyard. It is patterned after one belonging to the King of*

> *Siam, on which wall-scenes incident to a Mahometan Paradise will be in evidence. When this boat shall have been launched, water-nymphs and siren sounds will surely increase the ever-present gaity on our river, which is already bringing about so much fun as caused by females of Alexandria. This will add to the many floating Monte Carlos and the music by our anchored excursion steamers nearby.*

The good times came to a close during the Great Depression, when the industry seemed to sail away along with the expendable cash that kept the business afloat. Stories of floating brothels operating into the 1960s can be heard around Old Town, although it can be hard to determine fact from fiction. The last known ark was discovered accidentally in 1993, when the Alexandria government was preparing to demolish an old, dilapidated marina office at the Old Town Yacht Basin. Workers discovered a shack that was part of a wooden barge sitting on a pile of dirt.

"City historians quickly arrived and declared it an ark, probably built around 1900, and the only known survivor among the thousands of houseboats, gambling barges and floating brothels that lined the Potomac River from the Civil War to after World War II," wrote journalist Paul Hodge in the *Washington Post*.

The city of Alexandria gave the ark to the Alexandria Seaport Foundation, a nonprofit organization that teaches shipbuilding skills to wayward youth. The ark is currently docked between Thompson's Alley and the foot of Queen Street, although the city's controversial waterfront plan includes language about moving it to the foot of Duke Street.

Bibliography

Chapter 1

Blanton, Wyndham B. "Washington's Medical Knowledge and Its Sources." *Annals of Medical History* 4 (1932): 52–61.

Boyd, Thomas. "Death of a Hero, Death of a Friend: George Washington's Last Hours." *Virginia Cavalcade* (Winter 1984).

Knox, J.H. Mason, Jr. "The Medical History of George Washington, His Physicians, Friends and Advisers." *Bulletin of the Institute of the History of Medicine* 1 (1933): 174–91.

Lear, Tobias. "Narrative Accounts of the Death of George Washington." December 14–15,1799.

Morens, David. "Death of a President." *New England Journal of Medicine* 341, no. 24 (December 1999).

Pirruccello, Frank. "How the Doctors Killed George Washington." *Chicago Tribune*, February 20, 1977.

Chapter 2

Burchard, Hank. "Army Stops Nazi Burial of Rockwell in Culpeper." *Washington Post*, August 30, 1967.

———. "Nazi Tries to Attack Patler at Hearing." *Washington Post*, August 29, 1967.
———. "Racist Leader Could Be Nasty, Charming…or Pitiful: Tells of Awakening." *Washington Post*, August 26, 1967.
McBee, Susanna. "Bearded GWU Student 'Infiltrated' Arlington Nazis to Get Thesis Data." *Washington Post*, June 6, 1959.
Simonelli, Frederick J. "The American Nazi Party, 1958–1967." *The Historian* 57, no 3 (1995): 553+.
Washington Post. "Candidates for Top Virginia Posts Range from Forester to Lawyer." October 28, 1965.
———. "Foul in Right Field." April 23, 1959.
———. "Jury Asserts Rockwell is a Nuisance." April 22, 1959.

CHAPTER 3

Loudoun Mirror. "The Leesburg Poisoning Case," April 24, 1872.
———. "The Lloyd Poisoning Case: The Arraignment of the Prisoner." October 30, 1872
———. "The Lloyd Poisoning Case: Sudden Deaths of the Father and Four Children." April 17, 1872.
———. "The Lloyd Trial: Acquittal of the Prisoner." November 8, 1872.
Smith, Kathryn Gettings. "Exploring Leesburg: Guide to History and Architecture." Town of Leesburg, 2003.

CHAPTER 4

Birchfield, Stan. "Did Pocahontas Save Captain John Smith?" http://www.ces.clemson.edu/~stb/doc/pocahontas.html.
Clark, Thomas. *Simon Kenton, Kentucky Scout*. N.p.: Jesse Stuart Foundation, 1993.
Crain, Ray. *Simon Kenton, The Great Frontiersman*. N.p.: Main Graphics, 1992.
Eckert, Allan. *The Frontiersmen, Narratives of America*. Book 1. New York: Bantam Books, 1967.
Ellis, Edward. *The Life and Times of Col. Daniel Boone, Hunter, Soldier and Pioneer*. Philadelphia: Porter and Coates, 1884.

Kenton, Edna. *Simon Kenton, His Life and Period, 1755–1836*. N.p.: Kessinger Publishing, 2007.
McKnight, Charles. *Our Western Border.* Philadelphia: J.C. McCurdy and Co., 1875.
Roosevelt, Theodore. *The Winning of the West.* New York: G.P. Putnam's Sons, 1894.

CHAPTER 5

Brown, George. *A History of Prince William County*. N.p.: Historic Prince William, Inc., 2006.
Groome, H.C. *Fauquier During the Proprietorship*. Westminster, MD: Heritage Books, 2008.
Herndon, G. Melvin. *Tobacco in Colonial Virginia*. N.p.: Tradition Classics, 2013.
Sour, Barbara. *A Brief History of Simon Kenton*. Champaign County Historical Museum, n.d.
Wallenstein, Peter. *Cradle of America: Four Centuries of Virginia History*. Lawrence: University Press of Kansas, 2007.

CHAPTER 6

Banham, Russ. *The Fight for Fairfax*. Fairfax, VA: George Mason University Press, 2009.
Burchard, Hank. "Appeals Fail in 8 Fairfax Bribery Case." *Washington Post*, February 6, 1968.
Fairfax Times. "Claiborne Leigh, Former Dranesville Supervisor, Dies." March 21, 2001.
McLaughlin, Maurine. "Jury Picked in Fairfax Bribe Case." *Washington Post*, January 10, 1967.
Sullivan, Patricia. "John P. Parrish, 88; Figure In '60s Fairfax Bribe Case." *Washington Post*, April 24, 2008
———. "Robert Claude Cotton Jr., 84, Dies; Convicted Ex-Fairfax Supervisor." *Washington Post*, January 1, 2005.
Yenckel, James. "Fairfax Considers Seeking Profits of Bribery Rezonings." *Washington Post*, April 20, 1967.

CHAPTER 7

Barber, James. *Alexandria in the Civil War*. Lynchburg, VA: H.E. Howard, Inc., 1988.

Kaye, Ruth Lincoln. *The History of St. Paul's Episcopal Church*. Springfield, VA: Goetz Printing Company, 1984.

Kunkahl, George. *Alexandria Goes to War: Beyond Robert E. Lee*. Knoxville: University of Tennessee Press, 2004.

CHAPTER 8

Ball, Frank. "The Arlington I Have Known." *Arlington Historical Magazine* (1964).

Foster, Jack Hamilton. "Crandal Mackey, Crusading Commonwealth's Attorney." *Arlington Historical Magazine* (1958).

Mackey, Crandal. *Brief History of Alexandria County, Virginia*. Falls Church, VA: Newell Printing Company, 1907.

Montague, Ludwell Lee. *Historic Arlington*. Arlington, VA: Arlington County Historical Committee, 1968.

Pratt, Sherman. *Arlington County: A Modern History*. N.p., 1977.

Rose, Cornelia. *Arlington County, Virginia: A History*. Baltimore, MD: Port City Press, 1976.

Templeman, Eleanor Lee. *Arlington Heritage: Vignettes of a Virginia County*. N.p.: privately self-published, 1959.

CHAPTER 9

Rosania, Mary Ellen. "The 'Fire-Eater' and the General." *Northern Virginia Heritage* 4, no. 1 (February 1982).

Ward, Ruth M. "A Duel in Arlington." *Arlington Historical Magazine* 7, no. 1 (October 1959).

Weems, M.L. *God's Revenge Against Dueling*. Washington, D.C.: Gideon, 1820.

CHAPTER 10

Levey, Bob, and Jane Freundel Levey. *Washington Album*. Washington, D.C.: Washington Post Books, 2000.

Lowry, Thomas. *The Story the Soldiers Wouldn't Tell: Sex in the Civil War*. Mechanicsburg, PA: Stackpole Books, 1994.

Tilp, Frederick. *This Was Potomac River*. 1978.

Topping, Elizabeth. *What's a Poor Girl to Do? Prostitution in Mid-Nineteenth Century America*. Gettysburg, PA: Thomas Publications, 2001.

About the Author

Michael Lee Pope is an award-winning journalist who lives in Old Town Alexandria. He has reported for the WAMU 88.5 News, the *Alexandria Gazette Packet*, the *New York Daily News* and the *Tallahassee Democrat*. A native of Moultrie, Georgia, he grew up in Durham, North Carolina, and graduated from high school in Tampa, Florida. He has a master's degree in American studies from Florida State University, and he lives in the Yates Gardens neighborhood with his lovely wife, Hope Nelson.

Courtesy of Liz Lynch.

Visit us at
www.historypress.net

This title is also available as an e-book